Efficient Building Design Series
Volume II

Heating, Ventilating, and Air Conditioning

J. Trost

Merrill
Prentice Hall

Prentice Hall
Upper Saddle River, New Jersey   *Columbus, Ohio*

Library of Congress Cataloging-in-Publication Data

Trost, J.
    Efficient building design series / J. Trost
      p.   cm.
    Includes index.
    Contents: v. 2. Heating, ventilating, and air conditioning
    ISBN 0-13-080336-7
    1. Building   I. Title.
   TH146.T64   1999   98–35394
   690—dc21   CIP

Cover art: © Ceri Fitzgerald
Editor: Ed Francis
Production Editor: Christine M. Harrington
Design Coordinator: Karrie M. Converse
Text Designer: Carlisle Publishers Services
Cover Designer: Ceri Fitzgerald
Production Manager: Patricia A. Tonneman
Marketing Manager: Danny Hoyt

This book was set in Cochin by Carlisle Communications, Ltd. and was printed and bound by Courier/Kendallville, Inc. The cover was printed by Phoenix Color Corp.

Printed in the United States of America

10 9 8 7 6 5 4 3 2

ISBN: 0-13-080336-7

Prentice-Hall International (UK) Limited, *London*
Prentice-Hall of Australia Pty. Limited, *Sydney*
Prentice-Hall Canada Inc., *Toronto*
Prentice-Hall Hispanoamericana, S.A., *Mexico*
Prentice-Hall of India Private Limited, *New Delhi*
Prentice-Hall of Japan, Inc., *Tokyo*
Pearson Education Asia Pte. Ltd., *Singapore*
Editora Prentice-Hall do Brasil, Ltda., *Rio de Janeiro*

PREFACE

If you were taken on board a ship which went . . . with a strong tide before a following wind, you would undoubtedly be much impressed with the power of that ship. You would be wrong; and yet in a way you would also be right, for the power of the waters and the wind might be said rightly to belong to the ship, since she had managed, alone amongst all vessels, to ally herself with them.

Isak Dinesen, 1934

An efficient building, like Dinesen's ship, is a fine blend of knowledge, invention, and climate. Efficient buildings provide shelter and comfort by selectively using or resisting natural energy flows. The fuel and electrical energy required to operate a building during its useful life will usually cost more than the building's construction. Residential and commercial buildings account for more than one-third of U.S. energy consumption, and much of this energy is used for heating and cooling. The design decisions that shape a building also build a long-term demand for energy resources.

This book can help building designers, developers, constructors, managers, occupants, and owners to refine and improve their understanding of efficiency in building operation. Committed readers can expect to develop a working knowledge of the design decisions, equipment options, and operating costs associated with building heating-cooling systems. After completing the text, readers should be able to:

1. Quantify building heat losses and gains.
2. Describe heating-cooling equipment operation.
3. Size, select, and detail the components of building heating-cooling systems.
4. Integrate heating-cooling components with building structure and construction.
5. Evaluate energy-conserving opportunities and alternatives.

A secondary goal of the text is to respect your time, talent, and perception by presenting material in a concise and logical format. Illustrations are included with text to expand and reinforce the information presented, and actual building applications are emphasized for the topics covered. Study problems follow the chapters so that you can develop confidence in your ability to apply new knowledge and skills. Chapters 1 through 5 allow you to build a knowledge base concerning comfort, heat flow, building heating-cooling equipment, and system selection. Chapter 6 presents a method for predicting annual building heating-cooling costs, and Chapters 7 and 8 outline opportunities for designing efficient buildings based on a working knowledge of heat flow.

Finally, I appreciate the helpful comments and suggestions from the Prentice Hall reviewers for Volume II: D. Perry Achor, Purdue University; and Marcel Sammut, Architect and Structural Engineer.

CONTENTS

Contents

CHAPTER 1

Terms, Comfort, and Psychrometrics

The best I have to offer you is the small size of the mosquitoes.

Basho

———— ◦◉◦ ————

This is a small chapter, but it contains a surprisingly large quantity of information. The list of HVAC terms is the foundation of your ability to communicate effectively with professionals. The comfort section presents a brief overview of three ways that the human body maintains heat balance. Finally, the psychrometrics section introduces the interactions between heat, moisture, and air that affect comfort.

Start by reading through the terms twice. Read the definitions for R and HVAC three times because these terms are introduced in the psychrometrics discussion but they are explained in greater detail later in the text. Plan to return to this list as you complete each section to review and reinforce the new terms covered in your readings.

As you study the topic of comfort, realize that it is quite subjective, and one person's ideal may be another's minimum. Fortunately, there is a general consensus concerning thermal comfort, and most building occupant needs can be met with a quality HVAC system.

The psychrometrics section introduces a variety of new terms and concepts. Psychrometric considerations impact efficient buildings in three significant ways:

1. They establish the air quantities and duct sizes required for a given building.
2. They determine the cooling capacity required to control moisture.
3. Psychrometric calculations are also used to predict condensation problems that may damage building components.

Most applications for psychrometric calculations are developed in later chapters, but make sure you understand and can use the psychrometric chart by solving the example problems that follow this chapter.

———— ◦◉◦ ————

1

1.0 HVAC TERMS

Most professions use special terms (jargon) to describe the concepts and equipment they work with; this special language may also help ensure future income. To work and communicate effectively with building heating-cooling professionals you must learn and speak their language. Reading this list before you begin the text and reviewing it after each chapter will establish a professional language foundation and permit you to communicate with the individuals who construct and equip your buildings.

Air-conditioning   Controlling air temperature, humidity, and quality.

Absorption   A refrigeration cycle where input energy is heat.

Adiabatic   Without gain or loss of heat.

Air-cooled condenser   A heat exchanger that transfers building heat to outdoor air.

Air handler   Air-moving equipment that can change air temperature, humidity, and quality.

BTU   British thermal unit. Quantity of heat. One BTU will increase the temperature of 1 pound of water 1°F (1 Calorie = 4 BTU).

BTUH   Rate of heat flow. BTU per hour.

C   The tendency to conduct heat for a standard thickness of material. *See* **U**.

CFM   Cubic feet per minute. Quantity of air.

Chiller   A heat exchanger where an evaporating refrigerant chills water.

Chill water   Water at about 45°F used in a heat exchanger to cool and dehumidify an air stream.

Coil   A heat exchanger (e.g., cooling coil).

Cooling tower   A heat exchanger that transfers building heat to outdoor air by evaporating water.

Condensation   Change of state from vapor to liquid; heat is released.

Constant volume   HVAC equipment that controls room temperature by controlling the temperature of conditioned air.

COP   Coefficient of performance. An efficiency rating for heating (cooling) equipment. BTU delivered (removed) divided by input BTU.

Deck   A heat exchanger (i.e., hot deck, cold deck).

Dehumidify   Remove moisture.

Dry-bulb temperature   Temperature indicated by a standard thermometer.

DX   Direct expansion. Equipment that uses an evaporating refrigerant to cool air.

Economizer   Cooling with outdoor air.

Emissivity   Tendency of a surface to radiate heat.

Enthalpy   Total heat in an air/water vapor mixture.

Entropy   Tendency toward uniform inertness.

Evaporation   Change of state from liquid to vapor.

Evaporator   A heat exchanger where evaporating refrigerant cools an air stream.

FPM   Feet per minute. Velocity.

GPM   Gallons per minute. Quantity of fluid flow.

Grain   1/7,000 of a pound.

Head   Total mechanical energy in a fluid at a point in a piping system.

Heat exchanger   A device that transfers heat from one fluid to another.

Heat pump   A reversible refrigeration machine.

HSPF   Heating seasonal performance factor. The number of BTUs per watt delivered by a heat pump.

Humidify   Add moisture to air.

HVAC   Heating, ventilation, and air-conditioning.

Hydronic   Equipment that circulates water to move heat.

Inches of water   Units for measuring pressure in fan and duct systems.

Infiltration   Air that leaks into a building.

k   Tendency to conduct heat for a 1-inch thickness of material. *See* **U**.

kW   Kilowatt. 1,000 watts of electrical energy. One kW = 3,400 BTU.

Latent heat   Hidden heat, absorbed or released when water changes state (liquid—vapor).

Psychrometrics   Properties of air/water vapor mixtures.

R   Resistance. Tendency to resist heat flow. R = 1/C or 1/k. *See* **U**.

Refrigeration   Moving heat from a cool location to a warm location.

Relative humidity   A measure of water vapor held by air; 100% relative humidity is a saturated air/water vapor mixture.

SEER   Seasonal energy efficiency ratio. A cooling efficiency rating for air conditioners and heat pumps. The number of BTU removed by each watt of energy input.

Sensible heat   Dry heat, as measured by a dry-bulb thermometer.

Specific heat   Number of BTU that will increase the temperature of 1 pound of a substance 1°F.

Sq. ft.   Square feet. Area.

Strip heat   Electric resistance heating.

Throw   Horizontal distance an air stream travels.

Ton   12,000 BTUH cooling effect.

U   The tendency of a construction to conduct heat. The number of BTU that will be conducted through one sq. ft. of a construction when the temperature difference across the construction is 1°F ($U = 1/R_t$).

Variable volume   HVAC equipment that controls room temperature by controlling the quantity of conditioned air.

Ventilation   Outside air brought into a building.

Watt   A quantity of electrical energy. About 10 BTU are required to produce a watt at power plants. In a toaster or water heater, 1 watt yields 3.4 BTU. In an air conditioner or heat pump, 1 watt can move 8-16 BTU.

Wet-bulb temperature   Temperature indicated by a thermometer when water is evaporating from a wet sleeve attached to the thermometer bulb. Wet-bulb temperature is an indicator of the total heat in an air/water vapor mixture.

Zone   A group of similar spaces or rooms.

1.1 COMFORT

Comfort criteria for buildings have been developed for "Sedoc," an imaginary lightly clothed "sedentary occupant." (See Figure 1.1.) Surveys show most people prefer 70°F in winter and 75°F in summer, but authorities recommend 65°F in winter and 80°F in summer as comfortable and economical indoor temperatures. This text uses 70°F in winter and 75°F in summer to select heating and air-conditioning equipment. Occupants may then adjust indoor temperatures as desired for comfort or energy conservation.

Physical comfort requires continuing dissipation of body heat by:

1. Convection
2. Radiation
3. Evaporation

Convection is circulation of liquids or gasses caused by temperature difference. When air temperature is less than skin surface temperature, body heat can be lost by convection to the surrounding air. Increased air motion will increase convective heat losses.

Radiation is heat transfer by electromagnetic wave, from a warmer to a cooler surface. Body surfaces radiate heat to cooler surroundings and receive radiant heat from warmer surroundings. The magnitude of radiant heat flow is dependent on the temperature difference between source and receiver. Radiant heat flow situations in buildings often involve windows. Winter window surface temperatures can be 25°F below room air temperature causing uncomfortable areas near windows.

Evaporation is a change of state from liquid to vapor. The human body continually dissipates heat by evaporation. Water vapor is expelled with each breath, and the evaporation rate can be increased by increased respiration or by perspiration. Humidity, the amount of water vapor in air, can affect comfort. However, the human body tolerates a wide range of humidity before becoming uncomfortable in very wet or very dry air.

Heat can also be lost by conduction (e.g., bare feet touching a cold floor) but most body heat losses are convective, radiant, or evaporative.

Some researchers spend a lifetime studying comfort, but exact results from such study are unlikely. Consider lightly clad skiers delighting in a brisk run through cold air and later enjoying total immersion in a tub of hot water (see Figure 1.2). The temperature of surroundings affects comfort, but so does activity, attitude, and clothing.

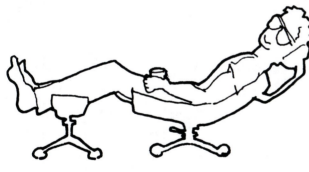

Sedoc

FIGURE 1.1

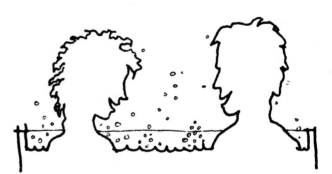

FIGURE 1.2

1.2 PSYCHROMETRICS

The psychrometric chart in Figure 1.3 describes air/water vapor mixtures; it can be used to predict condensation problems and to calculate HVAC capacity. Seven characteristics of air/water vapor mixtures are noted on the chart. If any two unrelated characteristics are known, the other five can be read.

1. **Dry-bulb temperature** The air temperature (°F) indicated by a standard thermometer.
2. **Percent relative humidity** The amount of water vapor held in the air as a percent of the maximum amount of water vapor the air can hold *at a specific temperature* (warmer air holds more water vapor).
3. **Wet-bulb temperature** The temperature (°F) indicated by a thermometer with a wet wick attached to its bulb; the wick is located in a moving air stream to encourage evaporation.

4. **Humidity ratio** The weight of water vapor held in 1 pound of dry air (weight is measured in grains; 1 grain = 1/7,000 of a pound).
5. **Dew point** The air temperature at which condensation begins.
6. **Enthalpy** The total heat contained in an air/water vapor mixture (BTU per pound of dry air).
7. **Specific volume** The number of cubic feet that 1 pound of air occupies.

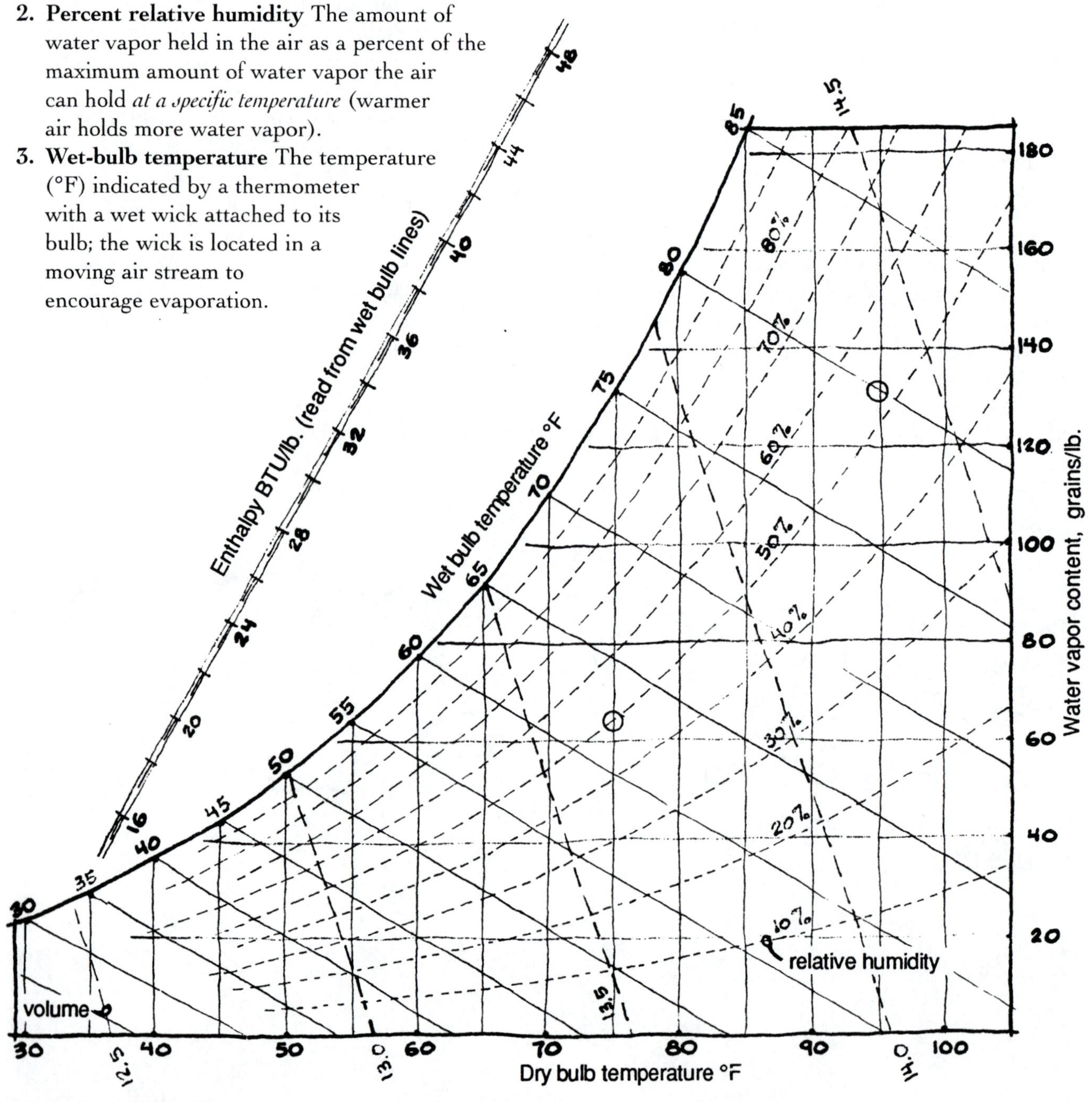

Psychrometric Chart

FIGURE 1.3

EXAMPLES

Use Figures 1.3 and 1.4 to:

1. Find the characteristics of an air/water vapor mixture at 75°F and 50% relative humidity.

2. Find the characteristics of an air/water vapor mixture at 95°F dry bulb, and 80°F wet bulb.

Characteristic	Example 1	Example 2
Dry-bulb temperature °F	**75**	**95**
Percent relative humidity	**50**	53
Wet-bulb temperature °F	63	**80**
Humidity ratio (grains)	65	132
Dew point °F	55	75
Enthalpy (BTU/lb)	28	44
Specific volume cubic feet/lb)	13.7	14.4

Notice that the 95° air/water vapor mixture contains twice as much water as the 75° mixture, but its relative humidity is nearly the same because warmer air can hold more water.

SENSIBLE HEAT, LATENT HEAT, AND ENTHALPY

HVAC equipment must deal with two kinds of heat. Sensible heat is the dry heat in air as measured by a dry-bulb thermometer. Latent heat is the heat held in water vapor. Heating equipment may include humidifiers which add moisture to dry winter air, and a large part of summer cooling energy is used to remove moisture from air. Enthalpy, the total heat in an air/water vapor mixture, is the sum of sensible plus latent heat.

The heating or cooling capacity required to produce sensible and latent changes in an air/water vapor mixture can be accurately predicted using data from the psychrometric chart. The following formulas apply and will be developed in the next chapter.

$$(CFM)(1.08)(TD) = BTUH \text{ sensible}$$
$$(CFM)(0.68)(GD) = BTUH \text{ latent}$$
$$(CFM)(4.5)(ED) = BTUH \text{ total}$$

CONDENSATION

When a building component's surface temperature is below the dew point of the surrounding air/water vapor mixture, condensation can occur. Such condensation is a common winter problem on single glass windows. In the next chapter you'll learn to calculate the surface temperature of windows and other building components so that condensation problems can be anticipated and corrected.

VAPOR BARRIERS

Many building materials are permeable, that is, water vapor can pass through them. Masonry, wood, sheet rock, and many insulations are permeable. Of

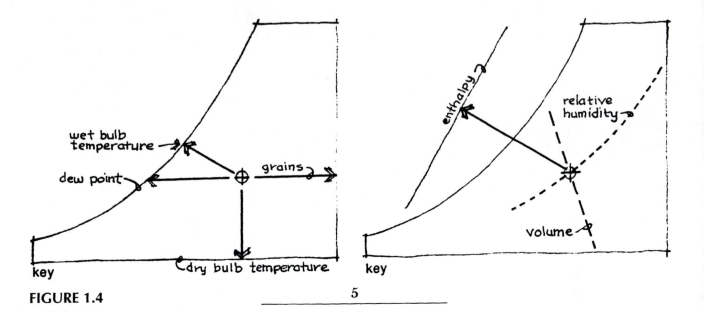

FIGURE 1.4

course, water vapor will pass through any of the small cracks, joints, or holes that often penetrate a building's skin.

Cold air cannot hold as much water vapor as warm air. The driving force for water vapor movement is vapor pressure difference, and cold outdoor air usually has a lower vapor pressure than heated indoor air. When water vapor passes through a wall or roof it will condense if it contacts a material whose temperature is below its dew point. Condensation inside a wall or roof construction can cause cosmetic and structural damage.

Vapor barriers include less permeable materials such as aluminum foil, plastic film, or waxed paper. They are installed on or near the **warm side** of a construction where they prevent vapor penetration and minimize internal condensation problems. Winter conditions usually govern building vapor barrier location, except in tropical climates or refrigeration work.

REVIEW PROBLEMS

Problems 1–10 deal with reading data from the psychrometric chart (see Figures 1.5 and 1.6), 11–17 test your understanding of the chart, and 18–20 are examples of applications in buildings.

READ

Find the dew point temperature for the following air/water vapor mixtures.

1. 75°F dry bulb, 60% RH (relative humidity)
2. 80°F dry bulb, 70°F wet bulb
3. 90°F dry bulb, 30% RH

Find the RH (relative humidity) of the following air/water vapor mixtures.

4. 70°F dry bulb, 50°F wet bulb
5. 90°F dry bulb, 80°F wet bulb

Find the water vapor content in grains per pound for the following air/water vapor mixtures.

6. 95°F dry bulb, 40% RH
7. 70°F dry bulb, 70°F wet bulb

Find the enthalpy in BTU per pound for the following air/water vapor mixtures.

8. 85°F dry bulb, 65°F wet bulb
9. 100°F dry bulb, 10% RH

Find the dry-bulb temperature in °F for the following air/water vapor mixture.

10. 65°F wet bulb, 30 BTU/lb enthalpy

THINK

Try to answer the following seven questions without looking at the psychrometric chart; if you understand the chart you can do it.

11. The two air/water vapor mixtures below have the same relative humidity. Which has the larger water vapor content in grains per pound? 90°F db, 40% RH; or 80°F db, 40% RH

12. The two air/water vapor mixtures below have the same dry-bulb temperature. Which one has the higher relative humidity? 80°F db, 60°F wb; or 80°F db, 50°F wb

13. The two air/water vapor mixtures below have the same relative humidity. Which one has the lower dew point temperature? 70°F db, 50% RH; or 80°F db, 50% RH

14. The two air/water vapor mixtures below have the same dew point temperature. Which one has the higher enthalpy? 80°F db, 50°F dp; or 90°F db, 50°F dp

15. The two air/water vapor mixtures below have the same dew point temperature. Which one has the greater moisture content in grains? 80°F db, 50°Fdp; or 90°F db, 50°F dp

16. The two air/water vapor mixtures below have the same wet-bulb temperature. Which one will have the lower dew point temperature? 90°F db, 70°F wb; or 80°F db, 70°F wb

17. Which air/water vapor mixture will occupy the larger volume? 90°F db, 70°F wb; or 80°F db, 70°F wb

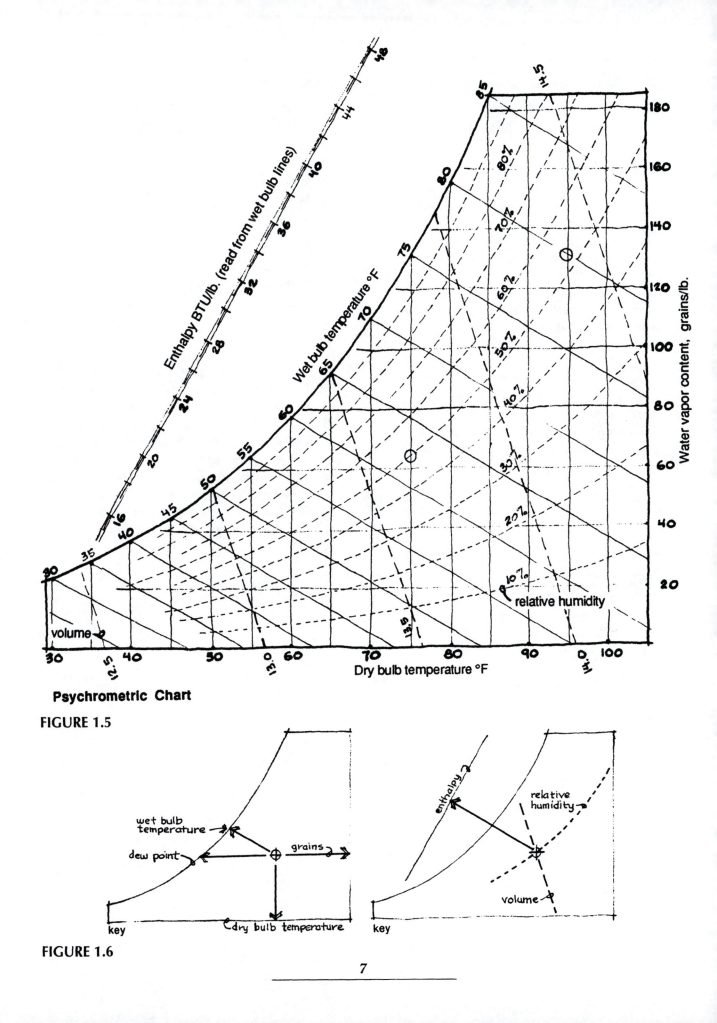

Psychrometric Chart

FIGURE 1.5

FIGURE 1.6

7

APPLICATIONS

These problems are similar to the preceding 17 but they are stated as actual building applications.

18. The air supply for heating a room can be provided at 90°F db, 40% RH **or** 95°F db, 25% RH. Which air supply will heat the room with the lowest quantity of supply air (and the smaller duct system)?

19. Identical buildings will be constructed in Phoenix and New Orleans; both will have separate air-conditioning units to cool outdoor air for ventilation purposes. If summer air in Phoenix is 105°F db, 20% RH; and summer air in New Orleans is 90°F db, 60% RH; which building requires larger cooling capacity?

20. The surface temperature of an uninsulated steel duct carrying conditioned air is 55°F. If the duct passes through a space where the air surrounding it is 78°F db, 50% RH; will moisture condense on the surface of the duct?

ANSWERS

1. 60°F
2. 65°F
3. 55°F
4. 20%
5. 65%
6. 100 grains
7. 110 grains
8. 30 BTU/lb
9. 29 BTU/lb
10. No answer; both givens read on the same line.
11. 90°F dry bulb, 40% RH, because warm air holds more moisture.
12. 80°F db, 60°F wb
13. 70°F db, 50% RH
14. 90°F db, 50°F dew point
15. Grains of water vapor are the same for both.
16. 90°F db, 70°F wb
17. 90°F db, 70°F wb
18. 90°F db, 40% RH. This air supply has the higher enthalpy (total heat) and therefore less of it is required to heat the example room.
19. New Orleans. Higher enthalpy in 90°F db, 60% RH air means more heat to be removed.
20. Yes. The duct surface is below the dew point temperature of the surrounding air.

CHAPTER 2

Heat Loss and Gain

*It is nice to read news that our spring
rain also visited your town.*

Onitsura

———————

When you complete this chapter you should be able to calculate heat loss and heat gain for residential or commercial buildings. This ability will enable you to size heating and cooling equipment. In Chapter 6 it will be used again as the basis of annual heating and cooling cost estimates.

Begin by learning about R values, U values, infiltration, and ventilation. These four factors are part of all heat loss and heat gain calculations so read to understand what they are and where to use them.

Next learn the two simple formulas that quantify building heat loss. The first deals with heat flow through a building's skin and the second concerns the outdoor air. A form is used to help organize heat loss calculations. Review it and then study the examples until you understand all the entries.

The heat gain analysis is done on the same form as heat loss because many aspects of both calculations repeat. However, summer heat gains differ from winter heat losses because they include added calculations covering solar, latent, and internal heat sources. Read to understand these differences and the five simple formulas that quantify them.

Finally, verify your new skills by doing the problems at the end of the chapter and by completing a new heat loss–heat gain summary form for a building of your choice.

The residence and the office building used for the example calculations will be reused in later chapters as discussion vehicles for equipment selection and annual operating cost estimates.

———————

2.0 HEAT FLOW

Heat flows downhill like water. "Downhill" for heat means from high temperature to low temperature. Temperature difference is the driving force for heat flow; greater temperature difference between regions means greater heat flow between them. Three types of heat flow can cause building heat loss or gain: conduction in solids, convection in fluids, and radiation between warm and cool objects. Heat is measured in **BTU** (British thermal units). A BTU is defined as the quantity of heat required to change the temperature of 1 pound of water 1°F.

INSULATION

A Thermos bottle is a good example of a device that resists all three types of heat flow. The only path for conducted heat flow is across the neck of the bottle. A vacuum between the walls prevents convective flow, and the reflective wall surfaces reduce heat transfer by radiation.

Insulation slows heat flow but does not stop it (see Figure 2.1). Most building insulations use many internal air spaces to limit conducted heat flow; polyurethane, fiberglass, and mineral wool are examples. Aluminum foil facing an air space can also be used as building insulation.

R IS RESISTANCE

Resistance values are an index of a material's tendency to resist heat flow. Larger R values mean more resistance.

R values are used as a starting point for calculating the rate of heat flow through a construction.* If you are evaluating heat flow through a wall made of brick and block, you begin by adding R(brick) plus R(block) to get R(wall). Since the wall is not in a vacuum, you will add a bit more R for air films that naturally form on wall surfaces.

---

*"Construction" is used to describe walls, ceilings, floors, etc., which may include several materials, air spaces, or air films.

drink fast
or
add R

U IS CONDUCTANCE

The reciprocal of the sum of the R values in a construction is called U.

$$U = \frac{1}{R_1 + R_2 + R_3 + \ldots}$$

U is an index of a construction's tendency to conduct heat. U is defined as the number of BTUs that will be conducted through 1 square foot of a construction in 1 hour when there is a 1°F temperature difference driving heat flow.

$$U = BTU/sq.\ ft./hr/°F$$

Calculate U for the wall shown:

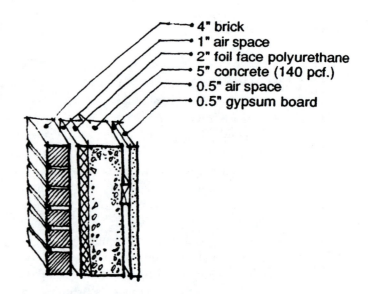

- 4" brick
- 1" air space
- 2" foil face polyurethane
- 5" concrete (140 pcf.)
- 0.5" air space
- 0.5" gypsum board

Rs		
	Air film outside	0.2
	4" brick	0.4
	Air space (facing foil)	3.0
	Polyurethane (2 × 6)	12.0
	Concrete (5 × 0.1)	0.5
	Air space	1.0
	Gypsum board (0.5 × 1)	0.5
	Air film inside	0.7
	R total	18.3

U value $U = 1/Rt = 1/18.3 = 0.054$

Do not confuse resistance to heat flow with heat storage capacity. Concrete is a poor insulator, but it has much more heat storage capacity than an equal volume of fiberglass. Heavy materials like concrete or masonry can be used to store heat and minimize indoor temperature changes from day to night.

FIGURE 2.1

2.1 R AND U VALUES
R VALUES FOR MATERIALS

The following are 1-inch thick unless noted otherwise.

Insulation	R per inch
Cellular glass	3
Cellulose	3–4
Mineral wool or fiberglass	3–4
Perlite	3
Polystyrene	4–5
Polyurethane	6
Polyisocyanurate Thermax	8
Vermiculite	2

Wood	
Plywood or softwoods	1.2
Hardwoods	0.9
OSB	0.9

Concrete	
Rock aggregate (140 pcf)	0.1
Perlite aggregate (40 pcf)	1.1

Other	
Earth (dry)	0.2
Earth (wet)	0.1
Gypsum board	1.0
Glass, steel, metals	Negligible

Masonry		R for thickness listed
Brick	4″	0.4
Concrete block	4″	0.7
(sand and	8″	2.0
gravel aggregate)	12″	2.3
Stucco or plaster	1″	0.1

Roofing	R for usual thickness
Shingles (asphalt)	0.4
Shingles (wood)	0.8
Built-up roof (tar and gravel)	0.3
Metal	Negligible

Air films	R for usual thickness
Outside building	0.2
Inside building	0.7

Air spaces	R for nominal 1″ space
Ordinary materials facing air space	1.0
Aluminum foil facing air space	3.0

U VALUES FOR CONSTRUCTIONS

U Values include air films

Walls

3 1/2″ wood studs, with exterior-type gypsum sheathing on both sides and no insulation	0.3
As above with R-11 insulation added	0.1
8″ concrete block (sand and gravel aggregate)	0.5
8″ concrete block with core insulation	0.3

Roofs	
No insulation	0.7
R-6 insulation	0.2
R-11 insulation	0.1

Windows	
Single glass	1.1
Single glass—low e	0.9
Double glass	0.6
Double glass-low e	0.3 to 0.4

Skylights	
Single glass or acrylic	1.2
Double glass or acrylic	0.7

Doors	
1 1/2″ solid core wood	0.5
As above with storm door added	0.3
1 1/2″ steel door with urethane core	0.2

Slab edge (heating ducts in slab)	
No insulation	1.0
1″ insulation	0.4
2″ insulation	0.2

Slab edge (no heating ducts in slab)	
No insulation	0.8
1″ insulation	0.3
2″ insulation	0.1

Note: Values given here are approximate (see Figure 2.2). They will change slightly with variations in material density, emissivity, temperature, and direction of heat flow. Try estimating a few R values for materials not listed here, and then check your estimates on pages 124–129. In the next section, R values are used to predict internal temperatures for an example wall.

0.412957 ?   try 0.4

FIGURE 2.2

INTERNAL TEMPERATURE

The temperature inside a wall or roof is an important consideration for vapor barrier location. Because insulation delays heat flow, the internal temperature distribution is not uniform; instead, it varies in proportion to a construction's R value. The following example wall and R values are repeated from the previous page. They will be used to illustrate temperature distribution within the wall.

Material	R
Air film outside	0.2
4″ brick	0.4
Air space facing foil	3.0
2″ polyurethane	12.0
5″ concrete	0.5
Air space	1.0
1/2″ gypsum board	0.5
Air film inside	0.7
R total	18.3

Example

Assume indoor temperature is 70°F and outdoor temperature is −10°F. The total temperature difference from inside to outside is 80°F. Begin by finding the temperature of the inside surface of the gypsum board wall.

The only thermal resistance (R) between the 70°F indoor air and the gypsum board surface is the inside air film with an R value of 0.7. The temperature difference between the indoor air and the gypsum board surface can be calculated as follows:

1. Multiply the indoor to outdoor temperature difference by 0.7 and then divide the total by the wall's total R value.

$$(80)(0.7) / 18.3 = 3°F$$

2. Since 3°F is the difference between the indoor air and the gypsum surface, the gypsum surface temperature is 70°F − 3°F = 67°F.

Now calculate the two missing in-wall temperatures that are marked (?) below.

Example Internal Temperatures	°F
Outside air	−10
Air film outside	−9
4″ brick	−7
Foil facing air space	?
2″ polyurethane	58
5″ concrete	?
1/2″ gypsum board	65
Air film inside	67
Inside air	70

Surface temperatures can affect occupant comfort as well as vapor barrier placement. If the interior surfaces of a room are much cooler than room air, people will feel uncomfortable because of increased radiant heat loss from the skin to cooler surrounding surfaces. Cold windows frequently cause such comfort problems. The academically correct description for this phenomenon is low MRT (mean radiant temperature).

2.2 INFILTRATION AND VENTILATION

Building air quality is maintained by introducing a continuous supply of "fresh" outdoor air. Reducing the fresh air supply will save heating and cooling dollars, but reductions may cause health problems and encourage "sick building" lawsuits. Current "fresh air" recommendations are 15 CFM (cubic feet per minute) per person or more for most building occupancies. Most homes rely on infiltration for fresh air while most commercial buildings are ventilated.

INFILTRATION

Infiltration describes air that leaks into a building because of construction quality, wind pressure, and temperature difference. Residences and small buildings often rely on infiltration to provide all necessary outdoor air. Special requirements such as cleaning, painting, or cooking odors are taken care of by opening doors and windows. Quantifying building infiltration is difficult because of the many variables involved. The estimates in Table 2.1 can be used in the absence of better information.

One air change per hour means that all the air in a building is replaced by outdoor air every hour. Since fan ratings and heating-cooling formulas are based on CFM, air change rates must be converted to CFM as shown in the following example.

Example

A room measures $9' \times 12' \times 8'$, and 1.5 air changes per hour are expected. Find outdoor air CFM for the room.

$$(volume)(air\ changes) \div 60\ minutes\ per\ hour = CFM$$
$$(9 \times 12 \times 8)(1.5) \div 60 = 21.6\ CFM$$

VENTILATION

Ventilation refers to air brought into a building by fans or designed apertures. In large buildings with few operable windows, ventilation is necessary to ensure healthy and odor-free conditions. The quantity of ventilation air brought into a building is determined by the number of occupants and their activities. The recommendations in Table 2.2 can be used in the absence of better information to estimate re-

TABLE 2.1

Building Description	Air Changes per Hour	
	Winter	*Summer*
No insulation, many operable windows and doors	3.0	2.0
Insulated walls and roof, built between 1945 and 1972	1.5	1.0
Well insulated and sealed, a residence built after 1972 or a commercial building without operable windows	0.75	0.5

Winter air changes are 50% larger than summer because of wind and air temperature difference.

TABLE 2.2

Ventilation Recommendations

Allow 15 CFM per person for most spaces, but increase or adjust as noted below.

Space Description	*CFM/Person*
Conference rooms	20
Dining rooms	20
Lobbies	20
Offices	20
Beauty shop	25
Hospital, patient room	25
Public rest rooms	50

Space Description	*CFM/sq. ft.*
Warehouse	0.05
Retail store	0.20–0.30
Locker rooms	0.50
Pet shops	1.00

Where smoking is permitted, allow 40–50 CFM/person.
In hotels, allow 30 CFM for bedroom plus 35 CFM for bath.

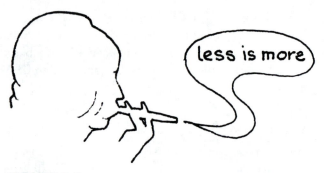

FIGURE 2.3

quired ventilation CFM. Use the maximum number of people expected to occupy the room or building as a multiplier (see Figure 2.3).

INFILTRATION OR VENTILATION?

Estimate infiltration and ventilation air quantities for a 10,000 sq. ft. school classroom building built in 1954. The conditioned space is 12 feet high, and the total population is 320 students and teachers.

Infiltration CFM. Estimate 1.5 air changes in winter and 1 air change in summer.

$(12)(10,000)(1.5) \div 60 = 3,000$ CFM in winter

$(12)(10,000)(1.0) \div 60 = 2,000$ CFM in summer

Ventilation CFM. Estimate 15 CFM per person.

$(15)(320) = 4,800$ CFM all year

Allow for heating and cooling capacity to satisfy the *larger* fresh air requirement—4,800 CFM of ventilation air for the classroom building.*

EFFICIENCY AND OUTDOOR AIR

Because it's expensive to heat or cool outdoor air, efficient buildings conserve energy by:

1. Minimizing outdoor air quantities.
2. Using heat exchangers to temper outdoor air.
3. Using an "economizer" instead of refrigeration equipment.

Minimize

Minimum outdoor air means minimum heating and cooling costs. Tight buildings with carefully controlled ventilation rates can save heating and cooling energy. Appropriate design strategies include quality construction and provision for reduced outdoor air on nights or weekends or whenever building occupancy drops.

Heat Exchangers

When outdoor air is brought into a building, it displaces conditioned air. Efficient buildings include heat exchangers to transfer heat between exhaust air and incoming outdoor air. Heat exchangers permit building operators to use outdoor air for odor control without paying the full price of heating or cooling it.

Economizer

Many large buildings are heat rich. The heat from lights, people, and computers can exceed building heating requirements on moderate winter days. Such buildings operate air-conditioning equipment in the winter to remove internal heat.

Economizer describes air intakes and dampers that permit the use of outdoor air instead of refrigeration for building cooling when outdoor temperature conditions are right. Even better is an enthalpy controlled economizer which evaluates both outdoor temperature and humidity, and then mixes appropriate quantities of outdoor and indoor air to achieve comfortable conditions without refrigeration.

---

*Ventilation fans pressurize the building and thus overcome anticipated infiltration. More conservative designers add infiltration and ventilation CFM to allow for exhaust fans and door openings.

2.3 ESTIMATING BUILDING HEAT LOSSES

A building's largest or "peak" heat loss is calculated to determine the size of heating equipment. Peak heat loss values will also be used in Chapter 6 to estimate annual operating costs and savings potential for energy-conserving alternatives. Heat leaves a building by only two routes: the building's skin conducts heat to colder outdoor surroundings, and cold outdoor air replaces heated building air.

CONDUCTED HEAT LOSSES

All parts of a building's skin lose heat to colder surroundings, and the rate of heat loss is determined by the U value of the skin. U is the number of BTUH conducted through 1 sq. ft. of a construction when a 1°F temperature difference drives heat flow. Conducted heat losses are given by the formula:

$$(U)(A)(TD) = BTUH$$

U   Conductance value in BTUH/sq. ft./°F
A   Area in sq. ft.
TD   Temperature difference between indoor and outdoor
BTUH   Rate of heat flow, BTU per hour

Each construction (wall, roof etc) with a unique area and U value is calculated separately and then the losses are summed to establish total building conducted heat losses. Since peak heat loss is used to size heating equipment the outdoor temperature is selected for a typical cold winter night.

OUTDOOR AIR HEAT LOSSES

Cold winter air leaks into a building through doors, windows, and many other small openings found in the skin of a typical building. Well-sealed buildings constantly exhaust indoor air and replace it with outdoor air to maintain air quality. To ensure comfortable indoor conditions, heating equipment must be sized with adequate capacity to heat this air. The following formula establishes the magnitude of heat losses caused by infiltration or ventilation air:

$$(CFM)(1.08)(TD) = BTUH$$

CFM   Quantity of outdoor air brought into a building by infiltration and/or ventilation in cubic feet per minute
1.08*   Number of BTUH required to increase the temperature of 1 CFM by 1°F*
TD   Temperature difference between indoor and outdoor air in °F
BTUH   Rate of heat flow, BTU per hour

Heat losses calculated by this formula are added to conducted heat losses through the building skin to establish total building heat loss.

Conducted Examples

1. Find the heat loss through a 200 sq. ft. window if its U value is 1.1, the indoor temperature is 70°F, and the outdoor temperature is 10°F.

$$(U)(A)(TD) = BTUH$$
$$(1.1)(200)(70-10) = \textbf{13,200 BTUH}$$

2. Find the heat loss through a 1,400 sq. ft. wall if its U value is 0.1, the indoor temperature is 70°F, and the outdoor temperature is 0°F.

$$(U)(A)(TD) = BTUH$$
$$(0.1)(1,400)(70-0) = \textbf{9,800 BTUH}$$

3. Find the heat loss through a 12,000 sq. ft. roof if its U value is 0.15, the indoor temperature is 70°F, and the outdoor temperature is 10°F.

$$(U)(A)(TD) = BTUH$$
$$(0.15)(12,000)(70-10) = \textbf{108,000 BTUH}$$

Outdoor Air Examples

4. A building has an expected infiltration rate of 400 CFM. Find the BTUH heat loss when the indoor temperature is 70°F and the outdoor temperature is −10°F.

$$(CFM)(1.08)(TD) = BTUH$$
$$(400)(1.08)(70-\{-10\}) = \textbf{34,560 BTUH}$$

---

*The constant 1.08 permits an answer in BTUH although fresh air quantity is in CFM.
1 CFM of air flow totals 60 cubic feet per hour, or 4.5 pounds per hour. Air has a specific heat of 0.24 BTU, so 0.24 BTU will increase the temperature of 1 pound of air 1°F. Therefore, (4.5)(0.24) = 1.08 BTUH are required to change the temperature of 1 CFM (60 CF/hr.) 1°F.

5. A building has an expected infiltration rate of 4,000 CFM *and* a ventilation rate of 6,000 CFM. Find the expected BTUH heat loss when the indoor temperature is 70°F and the outdoor temperature is 0°F.
Use the largest value for infiltration *or* ventilation (i.e., 6,000 CFM here).

$$(CFM)(1.08)(TD) = BTUH$$
$$(6,000)(1.08)(70-0) = \textbf{453,600 BTUH}$$

FOUR SPECIAL CASES OF HEAT LOSS

Three cases don't fit the preceding heat loss formulas. They are ducts outside conditioned spaces, basement walls and floors, and insulated but unheated spaces adjacent to conditioned spaces. A fourth case, slab edge losses, will fit with an allowance.

Ducts Outside

Heating ducts outside the conditioned space—in a vented attic, for example—can lose a lot of heat (see Figure 2.4). Often they carry 130°F air in an attic where the ambient temperature can be below 0°F, yet duct insulation may be only 1″ thick. Smart designers locate ducts inside the insulated zone; others add 10% to the sum of all other building heat losses to account for increased heat loss by the duct system.

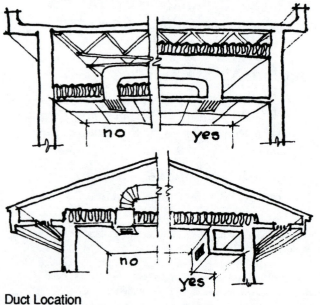

Duct Location
FIGURE 2.4

Basement Walls and Floors

Basement walls and floors in contact with the earth benefit from the earth's heat storage capacity and its resistance to heat flow (see Figure 2.5). To calculate heat loss through basement walls or floors (or slabs on grade) multiply the wall or floor area by the factor given in Table 2.3.

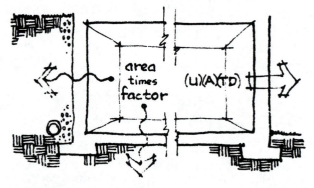

Basement Walls and Floors
FIGURE 2.5

TABLE 2.3

Design Temperature	Factor BTUH per sq. ft.
Over 10°F	2
Under 10°F	4

Note: For basement walls *not* in contact with earth, use the equation $(U)(A)(TD) = BTUH$.

Unheated Spaces

An insulated but unheated space adjacent to a heated space will delay heat loss (see Figure 2.6). Spare rooms, closed attics, and enclosed crawl spaces are examples. In these cases use the equation (U)(A)(TD) = BTUH, but reduce the TD by 50% to account for reduced heat flow.

Slab Edge

The formula (U)(A)(TD) = BTUH can be used to calculate heat loss through the exposed edge of concrete floor construction (see Figure 2.7). Allow 1 sq. ft. of area for each linear foot of slab edge.

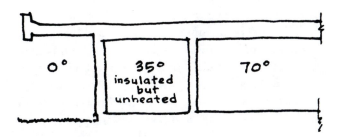

Unheated Spaces

FIGURE 2.6

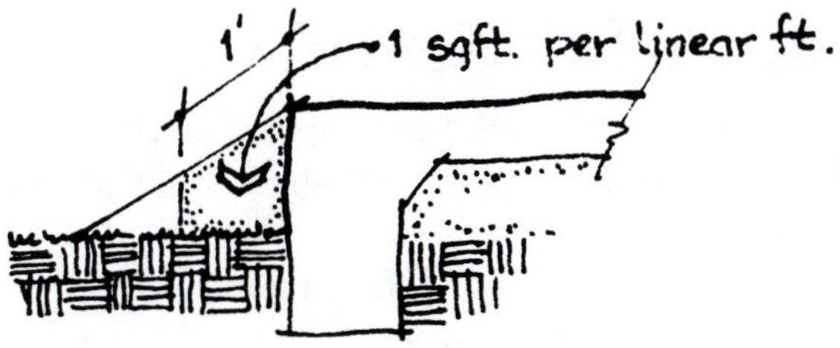

Slab Edge

FIGURE 2.7

2.4 CALCULATING BUILDING HEAT LOSS

The heat loss–heat gain summary form can be used to quantify peak heat loss (and later peak heat gain). Examine the form as you read this section; then work through the following examples. Heat loss calculations can be used to select heating equipment and to estimate annual heating costs.

DESIGN CONDITIONS: PROJECT CONDITIONS

Select winter outdoor temperature from the map in Figure 2.8 or refer to the current *ASHRAE Handbook of Fundamentals* for more precise data. The following examples use a winter indoor temperature of 70°F, but 65°F will conserve energy.

Fill in the appropriate project conditions blanks for the building you are evaluating.

QUANTITIES

Calculate and enter the quantities indicated in the left-hand vertical column of the form.

Outdoor air: Use the *larger value* for infiltration or ventilation. Refer back to pages 13 and 14 to estimate infiltration and ventilation CFM.
Glass: For heat loss, you need only the total glass area (subdivide this area into appropriate orientations for later calculations of heat gain). Enter skylights as "HOR" (horizontal) glass.
Lighting: Calculate peak heat loss without lighting; doing so ensures adequate heating capacity to warm the building on a cold night.

People: Calculate peak heat loss without occupants because they may arrive late on a cold night.
Ceiling-roof, walls: Remember to deduct window and skylight areas. If your building has a variety of roof or wall constructions, develop an average U value.
Floor: Use only the appropriate construction type.
Slab edge: Use linear feet here.

CALCULATIONS

After entering quantities, insert the appropriate U, TD, or factor values in the winter heat loss column and complete the multiplications indicated. Your BTUH total is the minimum size needed for the heating plant, and it can be used to estimate annual heating costs. For typical buildings in the United States the total heat loss should range between 20 and 60 BTUH per square foot of heated floor area (lower BTUH in the South, and higher in the North).

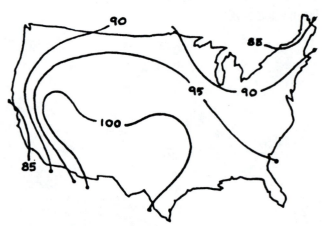

Summer design temperature °F (dry bulb)

FIGURE 2.9

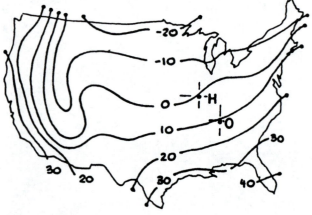

Winter design temperature °F (dry bulb)

FIGURE 2.8

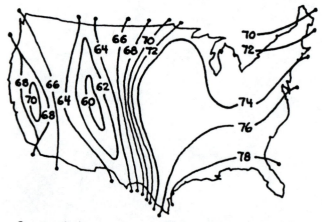

Summer design temperature °F (wet bulb)

FIGURE 2.10

_____ _____ _____ _____ _____
project name   location   floor area sqft.   calculated by   date

Design Conditions: **Project Conditions:**

winter   Outdoor Air; calculate 1&2 below but use only the <u>largest CFM</u> value:
____ °Fdb indoor   1. Infiltration based on air change rate_____winter _____summer
____ °Fdb outdoor   2. Ventilation based on CFM per person _____
____ T D
summer   Glass _____U value_____SC (Shading Coefficient)
____ °Fdb outdoor   Lighting _____ total watts operating at peak heat gain time
____ °Fdb indoor   People _____total occupants at peak heat gain time
____ T D   Ceiling-Roof _____U value _____color _____weight (lbs/sqft)
____ °Fwb outdoor   Walls _____U value _____color _____ weight (lbs/sqft)
____ % RH indoor   Floor _____U value, Door _____U value, Slab Edge U value _____
____ GD   Equipment _____watts or hp, Appliances _____
____ time of peak gain   Other _____

Item	Quantities	Winter Heat Loss = BTUH	Summer Heat Gain = BTUH
Outdoor Air			
winter	_____CFM	(1.08)(___TD) = _____	
summer	_____CFM		(1.08)(___TD) = _____
			(0.68)(___GD) = _____
Glass total	_____sqft	(___U)(___TD) = _____	(___U)(___TD) = _____
N	_____sqft		(___SF)(___SC) = _____
E	_____sqft		(___SF)(___SC) = _____
S	_____sqft		(___SF)(___SC) = _____
W	_____sqft		(___SF)(___SC) = _____
HOR	_____sqft		(___SF)(___SC) = _____
Lighting	_____watts		(3.4) = _____
People	_____#		(___sens) = _____
			(___latent) = _____
Ceiling-Roof	_____sqft	(___U)(___TD) = _____	(___U)(___ETD) = _____
Walls	_____sqft	(___U)(___TD) = _____	(___U)(___ETD) = _____
Floor bsmt	_____sqft	(___factor) = _____	
slab	_____sqft	(___factor) = _____	
crawl space	_____sqft	(___U)(___TD) = _____	
above grade	_____sqft	(___U)(___TD) = _____	
Slab Edge	_____linft	(___U)(___TD) = _____	
Doors	_____sqft	(___U)(___TD) = _____	(___U)(___TD) = _____
Equipment	_____watts		(3.4) = _____
	_____hp		(2500) = _____
Appliances	_____		(___sensible) = _____
			(___latent) = _____
Other	_____	_____	_____

	Subtotals	_____	_____
If ducts are outside the conditioned space add 10%		_____	_____
TOTAL BTUH	heat loss	_____	heat gain _____

Check; heat loss = 20-60 BTUH persqft. (south to north); heat gain = 15-60 BTUH per sqft. (north to south). Allow 4% of area served for fan rooms, and 2% of gross building area for central plant equipment.

2.5 HOUSE EXAMPLE, HEAT LOSS CALCULATION

DESIGN CONDITIONS

Winter temperature is 0°F (for location "H" in Figure 2.8). An indoor temperature of 70°F is assumed; temperature difference (TD) is 70.

PROJECT CONDITIONS

Outdoor air: The example house in Figure 2.11 was built in 1966 and has many windows. Estimate 1.5 air changes in winter; then estimate a minimum ventilation rate of 15 CFM per person. (p. 13)

Glass: Windows are single glass. U = 1.1 (p. 11).

Ceiling-roof: Detail in Figure 2.12. U = 1/R total = 0.05.

$$[1/(0.7+19+0.6+0.7) = 1/21 = 0.05]$$

Note that R values for the plywood roof deck and the metal roofing were not included in the U calculation above because cold outside air will occupy the vented attic space between the roof deck and the top of the insulation. Also note that an air film R value of 0.7 was used for both air films. The R value of 0.2 for the outdoor air film is based on wind speed, and wind penetration of the vented attic space is not expected. (p. 11)

Wall: See detail in Figure 2.12. U = 1/R total = 0.07.

$$[1/(0.2+0.1+1+11+0.5+0.7) = 1/13.5 = 0.07]$$

The R value of 1 is for the air space created by the 1×4 wood stripping. (p. 11)

Floor: Slab on grade. Factor is 4 BTUH per sq. ft. because the design temperature is below 10°F. (p. 16)

Slab edge: U value for uninsulated slab edge is 0.8. (pp. 11 and 17)

Doors: 1 1/2" solid core; U = 0.5 (p. 11).

QUANTITIES

See plan and section in Figure 2.11 for dimensions.

Outdoor air: The largest value comes from infiltration:

$$(AC) (vol) \div 60 = CFM$$

$$(1.5) (14,000) \div 60 = 350 \text{ CFM}$$

The estimated house volume of 14,000 CF includes the high ceiling areas of the house.

Glass: 320 sq. ft. including high windows at roof (small numbers on plan are low window areas).

Ceiling-roof: 1,620 sq. ft. including allowance for roof slope.

Walls: 1,090 sq. ft. including high end wall, wall at clerestory windows, wall at entry, and one half of the garage wall (because the garage TD is half the indoor to outdoor TD). (p. 17)

Floor slab: 1,568 sq. ft.

Slab edge: 140 linear feet; excludes 28 feet at garage.

Doors: 30 sq. ft. (actually 40 sq. ft. but the door to the garage has only half TD, so count half of this door area).

WINTER HEAT LOSS = BTUH

Insert appropriate U values, constants, factors, and temperature difference; then complete all multiplications and total the heat loss BTUH. Add 10% if ducts are located in an unconditioned attic.

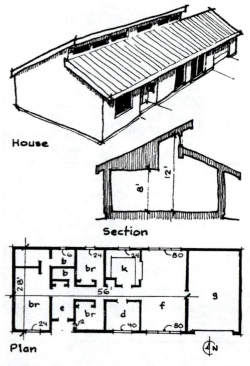

House

Section

Plan

FIGURE 2.11

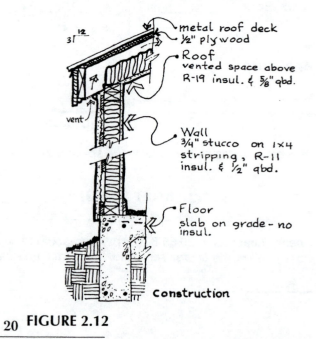

metal roof deck
½" plywood

Roof
vented space above
R-19 insul. & ⅝" gbd.

vent

Wall
¾" stucco on 1×4
stripping, R-11
insul. & ½" gbd.

Floor
slab on grade - no
insul.

Construction

FIGURE 2.12

House	*"H"* (map p. 18)	1,568	E J R	1·2·99
project name	location	floor area sqft.	calculated by	date

Design Conditions:

winter (p. 18)
70 °Fdb indoor
0 °Fdb outdoor
70 TD

summer
_____ °Fdb outdoor
_____ °Fdb indoor
_____ TD
_____ °Fwb outdoor
_____ % RH indoor
_____ GD
_____ time of peak gain

Project Conditions:

Outdoor Air; calculate 1&2 below but use only the **largest CFM** value:
1. Infiltration based on air change rate **350** winter _____ summer
2. Ventilation based on CFM per person **75** (5@15)

Glass **1.1** U value _____ SC (Shading Coefficient)
Lighting _____ total watts operating at peak heat gain time
People _____ total occupants at peak heat gain time
Ceiling-Roof **0.05** U value _____ color **6** weight (lbs/sqft)
Walls **0.07** U value _____ color **12** weight (lbs/sqft)
Floor **4** *factor* U value, Door **0.5** U value, Slab Edge U value **0.8**
Equipment _____ watts or hp, Appliances _____
Other _____

Item	Quantities	Winter Heat Loss = BTUH	Summer Heat Gain = BTUH
Outdoor Air			
winter	**350** CFM	(1.08)(**70** TD) = **26,460**	
summer	_____ CFM		(1.08)(_____ TD) = _____
			(0.68)(_____ GD) = _____
Glass total	**320** sqft	(**1.1** U)(**70** TD) = **24,640**	(_____ U)(_____ TD) = _____
N	_____ sqft		(_____ SF)(_____ SC) = _____
E	_____ sqft		(_____ SF)(_____ SC) = _____
S	_____ sqft		(_____ SF)(_____ SC) = _____
W	_____ sqft		(_____ SF)(_____ SC) = _____
HOR	_____ sqft		(_____ SF)(_____ SC) = _____
Lighting	_____ watts		(3.4) = _____
People	**5** #		(_____ sens) = _____
			(_____ latent) = _____
Ceiling-Roof	**1,620** sqft	(**0.05** U)(**70** TD) = **5,670**	(_____ U)(_____ ETD) = _____
Walls	**1,090** sqft	(**0.07** U)(**70** TD) = **5,341**	(_____ U)(_____ ETD) = _____
Floor bsmt	_____ sqft	(_____ factor) = _____	
slab	**1,568** sqft	(**4** factor) = **6,272**	
crawl space	_____ sqft	(_____ U)(_____ TD) = _____	
above grade	_____ sqft	(_____ U)(_____ TD) = _____	
Slab Edge	**140** linft	(**0.8** U)(**70** TD) = **7,840**	
Doors	**30** sqft	(**0.5** U)(**70** TD) = **1,050**	(_____ U)(_____ TD) = _____
Equipment	_____ watts		(3.4) = _____
	_____ hp		(2500) = _____
Appliances	_____		(_____ sensible) = _____
			(_____ latent) = _____
Other	_____	_____	_____

Subtotals	**77,273**	_____
If ducts are outside the conditioned space add 10%	*(inside)*	_____
TOTAL BTUH heat loss	**77,273**	heat gain _____

Check; heat loss = 20-60 BTUH persqft. (south to north); heat gain = 15-60 BTUH per sqft. (north to south). Allow 4% of area served for fan rooms, and 2% of gross building area for central plant equipment.

2.6 OFFICE EXAMPLE, HEAT LOSS CALCULATION

DESIGN CONDITIONS

Winter temperature is 10°F (for location "O" in Figure 2.8). An indoor temperature of 70°F is assumed; temperature difference (TD) is 60.

PROJECT CONDITIONS

Outdoor air: Estimate infiltration for the example office in Figure 2.13 at 0.75 air changes per hour in winter (0.5 air changes per hour in summer). Estimate ventilation rate at 15 CFM per person. Fresh air CFM due to infiltration is the largest value in winter. (pp. 13–14)

Glass: Double glass. U = 0.6 (p. 11).

Lighting: Do not take heat gain credit because lights will be off on cold nights.

People: Estimate 160 occupants, but do not take heat gain credit because people are absent on cold nights.

Ceiling-roof: Detail is shown in Figure 2.14. U = 1/R total = 0.05.

$$[1/(0.2+18+0.7) = 1/18.9 = 0.05] \text{ (p. 11)}$$

Wall: See detail in Figure 2.14. U = 1/R total = 0.07.

$$[1/(0.2+0.4+1+0.5+11+0.5+0.7) = 1/14.3 = 0.07]$$

Floor: Slab on grade. Factor is 2 BTUH per sq. ft. (p. 16)

Slab edge: Not shown. No insulation; no heating ducts. U = 0.8 (pp. 11 and 17).

Doors: Single glass. U = 1.1 (p. 11).

Equipment: Do not take a heat gain credit for equipment because it does not operate on cold nights.

Office 160 occupants

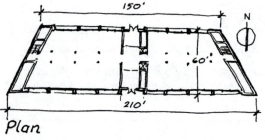

Plan

FIGURE 2.13   22

QUANTITIES

Refer again to Figures 2.13 and 2.14 for dimensions.

Outdoor air: Building volume is (21,600)(11) = 237,600 CF. At 0.75 air changes per hour the expected infiltration is (237,600÷60)(0.75)= 2,970 CFM. Ventilation rate for 160 people at 15 CFM each is 2,400 CFM. Use the larger infiltration value for winter heat loss. (pp. 13 and 14)

Glass: Windows are 4 feet high. Total window area is 2,400 sq. ft.

Ceiling-roof: Area is half floor area (two floors), 10,800 sq. ft.

Walls: Net wall is 10,880 sq. ft. Gross wall area is 10,950 sq. ft. Add for soffits and sills 2,400 sq. ft.; deduct for windows and doors 2,470 sq. ft.

Floor: Slab on grade area = 10,800 sq. ft.

Slab edge: 494 linear feet.

Doors: Two at 5'×7' = 70 sq. ft. (excluding fire exits—they are counted as wall area).

WINTER HEAT LOSS = BTUH

Insert appropriate U values, constants, factors, and temperature difference; then complete calculations and total heat loss BTUH. Add 10% only if ducts are outside the conditioned space.

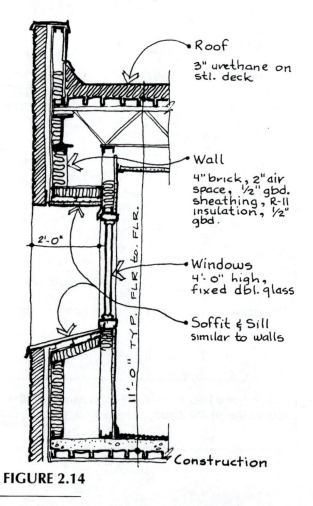

- Roof
  3" urethane on stl. deck

- Wall
  4" brick, 2" air space, ½" gbd. sheathing, R-11 insulation, ½" gbd.

- Windows
  4'-0" high, fixed dbl. glass

- Soffit & Sill
  similar to walls

2'-0"

11'-0" TYP. FLR. to FLR.

Construction

FIGURE 2.14

Office	"O" (map p.18)	21,600	GJ1A	1·3·99
project name	location	floor area sqft.	calculated by	date

Design Conditions:

winter *(p.18)*

70	°Fdb indoor
10	°Fdb outdoor
60	T D

summer

____	°Fdb outdoor
____	°Fdb indoor
____	T D
____	°Fwb outdoor
____	% RH indoor
____	G D
____	time of peak gain

Project Conditions:

3/4 A.C. .

Outdoor Air; calculate 1&2 below but use only the __largest CFM__ value:
1. Infiltration based on air change rate _2,970_ winter _____ summer
2. Ventilation based on CFM per person _2,400_ (160 @ 15) _____

Glass _0.6_ U value _____ SC (Shading Coefficient)
Lighting _____ total watts operating at peak heat gain time
People _160_ total occupants at peak heat gain time
Ceiling-Roof _0.05_ U value _____ color _____ weight (lbs/sqft)
Walls _0.07_ U value _____ color _____ weight (lbs/sqft) *glass doors*
factor → Floor _2_ U value, Door _1.1_ U value, Slab Edge U value _0.8_
Equipment _____ watts or hp, Appliances _____
Other _____

Item	Quantities	Winter Heat Loss = BTUH	Summer Heat Gain = BTUH
Outdoor Air			
winter	_2,970_ CFM	(1.08)(**60**TD) = _192,450_	
summer	_____ CFM		(1.08)(__TD) = _____
			(0.68)(__GD) = _____
Glass total	_2,400_ sqft	(**0.6**U)(**60**TD) = _86,400_	(__U)(__TD) = _____
N	_____ sqft		(__SF)(__SC) = _____
E	_____ sqft		(__SF)(__SC) = _____
S	_____ sqft		(__SF)(__SC) = _____
W	_____ sqft		(__SF)(__SC) = _____
HOR	_____ sqft		(__SF)(__SC) = _____
Lighting	_____ watts		(3.4) = _____
People	_____ #		(__sens) = _____
			(__latent) = _____
Ceiling-Roof	_10,800_ sqft	(**0.05**U)(**60**TD) = _32,400_	(__U)(__ETD) = _____
Walls	_10,880_ sqft	(**0.07**U)(**60**TD) = _45,700_	(__U)(__ETD) = _____
Floor bsmt	_____ sqft	(__factor) = _____	
slab	_10,800_ sqft	(_2_ factor) = _21,600_	
crawl space	_____ sqft	(__U)(__TD) = _____	
above grade	_____ sqft	(__U)(__TD) = _____	
Slab Edge	_494_ linft	(**0.8**U)(**60**TD) = _23,700_	(__U)(__TD) = _____
Doors	_70_ sqft	(**1.1**U)(**60**TD) = _4,600_	(3.4) = _____
Equipment	_____ watts		(2500) = _____
	_____ hp		(__sensible) = _____
Appliances	_____		(__latent) = _____
Other	_____	_____	
	Subtotals	_406,850_	_____
If ducts are outside the conditioned space add 10%		_inside_	_____
	TOTAL BTUH heat loss	_406,850_ heat gain	_____

Check; heat loss = 20-60 BTUH persqft. (south to north); heat gain = 15-60 BTUH per sqft. (north to south). Allow 4% of area served for fan rooms, and 2% of gross building area for central plant equipment.

2.7 ESTIMATING BUILDING HEAT GAINS

Many of the concepts developed for calculating heat loss also apply to heat gain. However, three added factors—sun, internal loads, and latent heat—make calculation of heat gain a bit more complex.

SUN

On a clear day the sun can radiate up to 350 BTUH on each square foot it reaches (see Figure 2.15). Radiant energy passes easily through glass, and it warms roofs and walls well above ambient air temperature. Since the sun is a moving heat source, its contribution to heat gain is continually changing, and a specific time must be used to estimate solar gain. Buildings will have different critical times for peak heat gain as a result of solar and occupancy factors. A church may experience peak heat gain at 11 AM, a gourmet restaurant at perhaps 9 PM, and an office building or residence at 4 PM. An office building with all windows facing southeast may peak at 10 AM.

Solar Heat Gain through Glass

Use the following equation to quantify solar gain through glass (see Figure 2.16):

$$(SF) \ (A) \ (SC) = BTUH$$

SF (solar factor) is the sun's output in BTUH per sq. ft.
A is the glass area in sq. ft.
SC (shading coefficient) is the percent of solar energy passing through the glass.
BTUH is the rate of heat flow in BTU per hour.

Note: Conducted heat gain through glass due to temperature difference occurs *in addition* to solar gain. The following equation is used to quantify conducted heat gain:

$$(U)(A)(TD) = BTUH$$

Heat Gain through Roofs and Walls

The sun can also increase the temperature of roofs and walls above ambient air temperature, and heat flow into the conditioned space is increased as a result. Heat gain through opaque roofs and walls may be calculated using the equation:

$$(U) \ (A) \ (ETD) = BTUH$$

U is the conductance value of the roof or wall in BTUH per sq. ft. per °F.

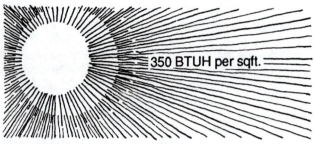

FIGURE 2.15

350 BTUH per sqft.

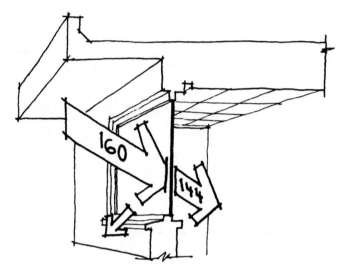

Solar BTU through glass

FIGURE 2.16

A is the area of roof or wall in sq. ft.
ETD (equivalent temperature difference) is an increased temperature difference which allows for heat gain caused by both air temperature difference and solar effect. ETD values will vary depending on the time of day, and the weight and color of the roof or wall.
BTUH is the rate of heat flow in BTU per hour.

Example

Use the tables in Section 2.8 to find the total heat gain through a 50 sq. ft. single-glass window facing southwest at 4 PM. The window is not shaded; its U value is 1.1 (p. 00). Outdoor temperature is 100°F and indoor temperature is 75°F.

$$(SF) \ (area) \ (SC) = solar \ gain$$
$$(160)(50)(90\%) = 7{,}200 \ BTUH$$
$$(U) \ (area) \ (TD) = conducted \ gain$$
$$(1.1)(50)(100{-}75) = 1{,}375 \ BTUH$$

Total heat gain 8,575 BTUH

Example

Use the tables in Section 2.8 to find the heat gain through a dark color 1,500 sq. ft. roof at 2 PM if the roof weight is 6 pounds per sq. ft. and the roof U value is 0.12.

$$(U)\,(area)\,(ETD) = total\ gain$$
$$(0.12)(1,500)(70) = 12,600\ BTUH$$

If the roof above is light color find heat gain.

$$7,560\ BTUH$$

If the roof is wet with water spray find heat gain.

$$2,700\ BTUH$$

INTERNAL LOADS

People, lights, appliances, motors, and food preparation add heat to building interiors. People and cooking can add both sensible (dry) and latent (wet) heat. Motors and lights add only sensible heat. HVAC equipment must remove internally generated heat to maintain comfortable interior conditions.

Example

Use the tables in Section 2.9 to find the total internal heat gain in a room caused by 10 people doing light work (standing), a 3 hp electric motor, and 12 light bulbs rated at 500 watts each.

(# people) (BTUH per person) = people gain	
(10) (750) =	7,500 BTUH
(hp) (2,500) = motor gain	
(3) (2,500) =	7,500 BTUH
(watts) (3.4) = lighting gain	
(12) (500) (3.4) =	20,400 BTUH
Total internal gain	35,400 BTUH

LATENT HEAT

Latent (phase change) heat exists in the water vapor carried by air (see Figure 2.17). As air temperature increases, its ability to carry water vapor increases. Significant air-conditioning capacity is required to dehumidify moist outdoor air because cool dry air is necessary for comfort. Calculate the air-conditioning capacity required to dehumidify outdoor air as follows:

$$(CFM)(0.68)(GD) = BTUH$$

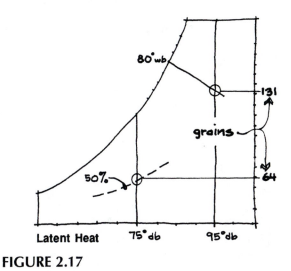

FIGURE 2.17

CFM (cubic feet per minute) is the quantity of moist air to be dehumidified.

0.68,* a constant, is the number of BTUH produced when 4.5 grains of water vapor condense (1 CFM = 60 CF per hr = 4.5 lb per hr; 1 grain per lb = 0.68 BTUH).

GD is the moisture difference in grains per pound of air between moist outdoor air and dry indoor air (1 grain = 0.00014 lb).

BTUH is the rate of heat flow in BTU per hour.

Example

Find the total heat gain caused by bringing 800 CFM of ventilation air into a building if the outdoor air is 95°F and 80°Fwb (wet-bulb temperature). Building air is 75°F and 50% RH (relative humidity).

$$(CFM)\,(0.68)\,(GD) = latent\ gain$$
$$(800)\,(0.68)\,(67) = 36,448\ BTUH$$

$$(CFM)\,(1.08)\,(TD) = sensible\ gain$$
$$(800)\,(1.08)\,(95\text{-}75) = 17,280\ BTUH$$

$$Total\ gain\ 53,728\ BTUH$$

Note that the total heat gain due to outdoor air includes both latent heat and sensible heat. The same equation used to quantify winter heat loss:

$$(CFM)(1.08)(TD) = BTUH$$

is used to quantify sensible heat gain.

---

*It takes 1,061 BTU to vaporize 1 pound of water at 212°F. This latent heat of vaporization is released when water condenses. Can you develop the latent heat formula constant—0.68?

2.8 SOLAR, SHADING, AND ETD VALUES

SOLAR FACTORS (SF)

The following BTU per hour per sq. ft. are based on clear day conditions.

Summer Values: July, Central U.S.

Solar Time	N	NE	E	SE	S	SW	W	NW	HOR
6 AM	40	120	140	70	10	10	10	10	30
8 AM	30	150	220	160	30	25	25	25	140
10 AM	35	60	150	160	80	35	35	35	230
Noon	40	40	40	80	110	80	40	40	260
2 PM	35	35	35	35	80	160	150	60	230
4 PM	30	25	25	25	30	160	220	150	140
6 PM	40	10	10	10	10	70	140	120	30
Clear day total	420	820	1,160	1,050	700	1,050	1,160	820	2,140

Winter Values: January, Central U.S.

Solar Time	N	NE	E	SE	S	SW	W	NW	HOR
8 AM	5	15	110	130	70	5	5	5	10
10 AM	15	15	120	240	210	50	15	15	100
Noon	20	20	20	180	250	180	20	20	130
2 PM	15	15	15	50	210	240	120	15	100
4 PM	5	5	5	5	5	70	130	110	15	10
Clear day total	120	130	500	1,170	1,600	1,170	500	130	700

Notes: Use *north* solar factors for glass with external shading; HOR = horizontal (e.g., a skylight).

SHADING COEFFICIENT (SC)

The following shows the percent of solar BTUH that pass through glass into the conditioned space.

Single glass (no blind)	90%	Double glass (no blind)	85%
Single glass with dark color drape or blind	70%	Double glass with dark color drape or blind	65%
Single glass with light color drape or blind	50%	Double glass with light color drape or blind	50%

Heat-absorbing, reflective, or low e glass can be as low as 10%. Refer to the manufacturer's specifications.

EQUIVALENT TEMPERATURE DIFFERENCE (ETD)

ETD accounts for solar radiation, mass, color, and air temperature difference.

Roof ETD: Dark Color, July, Central U.S.

Roof Weight (pounds per sq. ft.)	8 AM	10 AM	Noon	2 PM	4 PM	6 PM	8 PM
0–10	15	40	60	70	60	30	10
11–50	5	25	45	60	60	45	20
51 plus	5	10	25	40	50	50	40
Wet roof (spray or pond)	0	0	10	15	20	20	15

Note: Use **60%** of the values above for a **light color roof** (e.g., dark value = 50, light = 30).

Wall ETD: July, Central U.S.

To find ETD, add the following values to air *TD* for *only* the orientations listed below.

Lightweight walls—0 to 50 pounds/sq. ft.
    For light color, add 10 to the air TD value.
    For dark color, add 20 to the air TD value.

Heavyweight walls—over 50 pounds/sq. ft.
    For light color, use air TD value.
    For dark color, add 5 to air TD value.

	8 AM	10 AM	Noon	2 PM	4 PM	6 PM	8 PM
Wall orientation	NE	NE	E	S	SW	SW	NW
		E	SE	SW	W	W	
		SE				NW	

2.9 INTERNAL LOADS AND LATENT HEAT GAINS

INTERNAL LOADS

Internal loads include heat gains from lights, people, motors, kitchens, and other equipment.

Lighting

Lighting loads add heat to a building at the rate of 3.4 BTUH for each watt of lighting in operation. If lighting design is not complete use the following data to estimate total lighting watts.

Building Type	Watts per sq. ft. of Floor Area		Building Type	Watts per sq. ft. of Floor Area	
	Range	Average		Range	Average
Apartments	1–4	2	Residence	1–4	2
Church	0–2	1	Schools	1–4	2
Factories	2–8	3	Shopping center	1–10	3
Hospitals	1–4	2	Supermarket	2–5	3
Hotels	1–3	2	Retail shops	1–10	5
Libraries	1–4	2	Restaurant, fast	1–6	3
Offices	1–4	2	Restaurant, gourmet	0–1	1

Miscellaneous

Electric appliances or heaters: 3.4 BTUH per watt hour; motors 2,500 BTUH per hp hour.
Residential kitchens: Allow 1,200 BTUH (average value for all kitchen appliances).
Other equipment or appliances: Refer to manufacturers' nameplate data.

People: BTUH for Selected Activities	Sensible	Latent	Total
Sleeping	200	100	300
Seated (awake)	250	150	400
Standing	250	200	450
Standing (light work)	275	475	750
Dancing (quietly)	300	550	850
Walking (or exercise)	375	625	1,000
Bowling	575	875	1,450
Heavy work or basketball	650	1,150	1,800

LATENT LOADS

Grain Difference (GD): Per CFM of Ventilation or Infiltration Air

(Values assume 95°F outdoor and 75°F and 50% RH indoor; for greater accuracy refer to the psychometric chart on p. 5)

Outdoor °Fwb	GD	Outdoor °Fwb	GD
70°	5	76°	40
72°	15	78°	55
74°	27	80°	67

For example problems see pp. 6 and 26.

2.10 CALCULATING BUILDING HEAT GAIN

The heat loss–heat gain summary form can be used to quantify peak heat gain and peak heat loss. Examine the form as you read this section; then work through the following examples. Heat gain calculations can be used to select air-conditioning equipment and to estimate annual cooling costs.

DESIGN CONDITIONS: PROJECT CONDITIONS

Select summer outdoor dry-bulb temperature (°Fdb), and wet-bulb temperature (°Fwb) from the maps in Figures 2.18, 2.19, and 2.20, or refer to the current *ASHRAE Handbook of Fundamentals* for more precise data. The following examples use 75°Fdb and 50% relative humidity as comfortable indoor design conditions. GD (grain difference) is most accurate from the psychrometric chart but you can use the rough values when the outdoor design temperature is 95°F. The time of peak heat gain is 4 PM for most buildings, but churches may peak at 11 AM and dance halls at 11 PM so think a bit before selecting the time of peak gain or test several times to be sure. Fill in the appropriate project conditions blanks for the building you are evaluating.

QUANTITIES

Most quantities indicated in the left-hand vertical column of the form were filled in for the heat loss calculations (pp. 20 and 22). Comments below emphasize changes for heat gain.

Fresh air: Use the larger value for infiltration or ventilation; expected summer infiltration is 67% of winter infiltration (pp. 13 and 14).

Glass: Use the total glass area to calculate the conducted heat gain; then subdivide total glass area into appropriate compass orientations for calculating solar gain. Enter skylights as "HOR" (horizontal) or reverse glass.

Lighting: Enter the total watts of lighting that will be operating at peak heat gain time.

People: Enter the total number of people that will occupy the building at peak heat gain time.

Ceiling-roof, walls: Remember to deduct window and skylight areas. If your building has a variety of roof or wall constructions, develop an average U value.

CALCULATIONS

After entering quantities, insert the appropriate U, TD, ETD, and factor values in the summer heat gain column and complete the multiplications indicated. Your BTUH total is the minimum size needed for air-conditioning equipment, and it can be used to estimate annual cooling costs.

For typical buildings in the United States the total heat gain should range between 15 and 60 BTUH per square foot of air-conditioned floor area. Higher heat gains are for buildings with large internal heat loads.

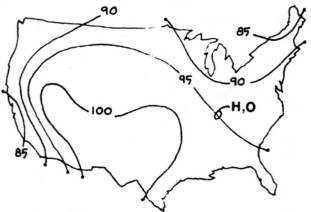

Summer design temperature °F (dry bulb)

FIGURE 2.19

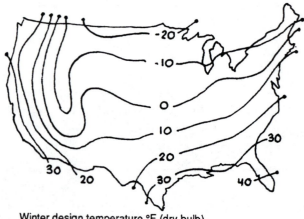

Winter design temperature °F (dry bulb)

FIGURE 2.18

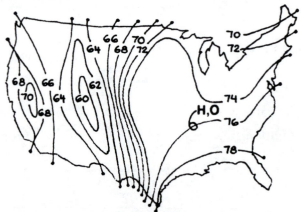

Summer design temperature °F (wet bulb)

FIGURE 2.20

| project name | location | floor area sqft. | calculated by | date |

Design Conditions:

Project Conditions:

winter

_____ °Fdb indoor
_____ °Fdb outdoor
_____ TD

summer

_____ °Fdb outdoor
_____ °Fdb indoor
_____ TD
_____ °Fwb outdoor
_____ % RH indoor
_____ GD
_____ time of peak gain

Outdoor Air; calculate 1&2 below but use only the **largest CFM** value:
1. Infiltration based on air change rate_____winter_____summer
2. Ventilation based on CFM per person _____

Glass _____U value_____SC (Shading Coefficient)
Lighting _____ total watts operating at peak heat gain time
People _____total occupants at peak heat gain time
Ceiling-Roof _____U value _____color _____weight (lbs/sqft)
Walls _____U value _____color _____ weight (lbs/sqft)
Floor _____U value, Door _____U value, Slab Edge U value _____
Equipment _____watts or hp, Appliances _____
Other _____

Item	Quantities	Winter Heat Loss = BTUH	Summer Heat Gain = BTUH
Outdoor Air			
winter	_____CFM	$(1.08)(\_\_TD) =$ _____	
summer	_____CFM		$(1.08)(\_\_TD) =$ _____
			$(0.68)(\_\_GD) =$ _____
Glass total	_____sqft	$(\_\_U)(\_\_TD) =$ _____	$(\_\_U)(\_\_TD) =$ _____
N	_____sqft		$(\_\_SF)(\_\_SC) =$ _____
E	_____sqft		$(\_\_SF)(\_\_SC) =$ _____
S	_____sqft		$(\_\_SF)(\_\_SC) =$ _____
W	_____sqft		$(\_\_SF)(\_\_SC) =$ _____
HOR	_____sqft		$(\_\_SF)(\_\_SC) =$ _____
Lighting	_____watts		$(3.4) =$ _____
People	_____#		$(\_\_\_\_sens) =$ _____
			$(\_\_\_\_latent) =$ _____
Ceiling-Roof	_____sqft	$(\_\_U)(\_\_TD) =$ _____	$(\_\_U)(\_\_ETD) =$ _____
Walls	_____sqft	$(\_\_U)(\_\_TD) =$ _____	$(\_\_U)(\_\_ETD) =$ _____
Floor bsmt	_____sqft	$(\_\_factor) =$ _____	
slab	_____sqft	$(\_\_factor) =$ _____	
crawl space	_____sqft	$(\_\_U)(\_\_TD) =$ _____	
above grade	_____sqft	$(\_\_U)(\_\_TD) =$ _____	
Slab Edge	_____linft	$(\_\_U)(\_\_TD) =$ _____	
Doors	_____sqft	$(\_\_U)(\_\_TD) =$ _____	$(\_\_U)(\_\_TD) =$ _____
Equipment	_____watts		$(3.4) =$ _____
	_____hp		$(2500) =$ _____
Appliances	_____		$(\_\_\_\_sensible) =$ _____
			$(\_\_\_\_latent) =$ _____
Other	_____	_____	_____

Subtotals	_____	_____

If ducts are outside the conditioned space add 10% _____   _____

TOTAL BTUH   heat loss _____   heat gain _____

Check; heat loss = 20-60 BTUH persqft. (south to north); heat gain = 15-60 BTUH per sqft. (north to south). Allow 4% of area served for fan rooms, and 2% of gross building area for central plant equipment.

2.11 HOUSE EXAMPLE, HEAT GAIN CALCULATION

DESIGN CONDITIONS

Maps show a summer dry-bulb temperature of 95°F and a wet-bulb temperature of 76°F (Figures 2.19 and 2.20, location "H"). Desired indoor conditions are 75°F and 50% relative humidity. Time of peak heat gain is estimated at 4 PM. Temperature difference (TD) = 20. Grain difference (GD) = 40 (p. 29). See Figure 2.21 for the example house plan. Refer to Figure 2.22 for construction details.

PROJECT CONDITIONS

Outdoor air: Select largest of infiltration at 1 air change per hour or ventilation at 15 CFM per person (pp. 13 and 14).

Glass: For single glass, U = 1.1. All windows have light colored draperies to reduce solar gain. Shading coefficient (SC) = 0.5 (p. 27).

Lighting: Negligible for a residence. At 4 PM, most lights will be off.

People: Use seated value for five occupants unless the house is used for exercise classes at 4 PM.

Ceiling-roof: U = 0.05; weight is 6 pounds per sq. ft.; color is dark; ETD is 60 (p. 28).

Walls: U = 0.07; weight is 12 pounds per sq. ft.; color is light; weighted average ETD is 22 (ETD = 30 for west wall, 20 for other walls; p. 11).

Floor and slab edge: No significant heat gain.

Doors: U = 0.5 (p. 11).

QUANTITIES

Outdoor air: One air change per hour at 235 CFM is more than the 75 CFM recommended for ventilation.

Glass: Of the total 320 sq. ft., 134 sq. ft. face north, 184 sq. ft. face south (includes clerestory), and 2 sq. ft. face west.

Ceiling-roof: 1,620 sq. ft. total including allowance for roof slope.

People: Each occupant produces 250 BTUH sensible plus 150 BTUH latent.

Walls: 1,090 sq. ft. (garage wall at 50%).

Doors: 30 sq. ft. (counting door to garage at 50%).

Appliances: 1,200 BTUH is an average allowance for residential heat gain due to appliances, cooking, showers, etc.

SUMMER HEAT GAIN = BTUH

Insert appropriate factors and temperature difference; then complete calculations and total BTUH. Add 10% if ducts are located in a hot attic.

Refer back to the heat loss example on page 20 if additional detail is needed.

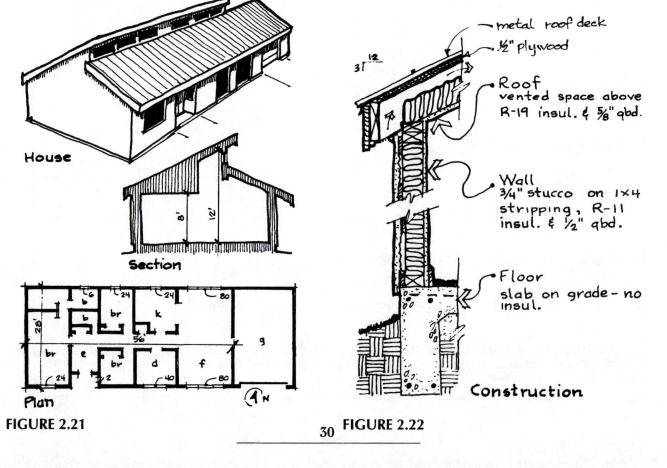

FIGURE 2.21

FIGURE 2.22

House	_"H"(map p.28)_	_1,568_	_EJB_	_1.2.99_
project name	location	floor area sqft.	calculated by	date

Design Conditions:

Project Conditions:

winter
- _70_ °Fdb indoor
- _0_ °Fdb outdoor
- _70_ TD

summer _(p.28)_
- _95_ °Fdb outdoor
- _75_ °Fdb indoor
- _20_ TD
- _76_ °Fwb outdoor
- _50_ % RH indoor
- _40_ GD _(p.27)_
- _4 P.M._ time of peak gain

Outdoor Air; calculate 1&2 below but use only the **largest CFM** value:
1. Infiltration based on air change rate _350_ winter _235_ summer
2. Ventilation based on CFM per person _75 (5@15)_ — _(2/3 of winter)_

light drapes

Glass _1.1_ U value _0.5_ SC (Shading Coefficient)
Lighting _—_ total watts operating at peak heat gain time
People _5_ total occupants at peak heat gain time
Ceiling-Roof _0.05_ U value _dark_ color _6_ weight (lbs/sqft)
Walls _0.07_ U value _light_ color _12_ weight (lbs/sqft)
Floor _4_ U value, Door _0.5_ U value, Slab Edge U value _0.8_
Equipment _____ watts or hp, Appliances _1,200_
Other _____ _residential kitchen_

Item	Quantities	Winter Heat Loss = BTUH	Summer Heat Gain = BTUH
Outdoor Air			
winter	_350_ CFM	(1.08)(_70_ TD) = _26,460_	
summer	_235_ CFM		(1.08)(_20_ TD) = _5,076_
			(0.68)(_40_ GD) = _6,392_
Glass total	_320_ sqft	(_1.1_ U)(_70_ TD) = _24,640_	(_1.1_ U)(_20_ TD) = _7,040_
N	_134_ sqft		(_30_ SF)(_0.5_ SC) = _2,010_
E	_____ sqft		(_____ SF)(_____ SC) = _____
S	_184_ sqft		(_30_ SF)(_0.5_ SC) = _2,760_
W	_2_ sqft		(_220_ SF)(_0.5_ SC) = _220_
HOR	_____ sqft		(_____ SF)(_____ SC) = _____
Lighting	_____ watts		(3.4) = _____
People	_5_ #		(_250_ sens) = _1,250_
			(_150_ latent) = _750_
Ceiling-Roof	_1,620_ sqft	(_0.05_ U)(_70_ TD) = _____	(_0.05_ U)(_60_ ETD) = _4,860_
Walls	_1,090_ sqft	(_0.07_ U)(_70_ TD) = _____	(_0.07_ U)(_22_ ETD) = _1,679_
Floor bsmt	_____ sqft	(_____ factor) = _____	
slab	_1,568_ sqft	(_4_ factor) = _6,272_	
crawl space	_____ sqft	(_____ U)(_____ TD) = _____	
above grade	_____ sqft	(_____ U)(_____ TD) = _____	
Slab Edge	_140_ linft	(_0.8_ U)(_70_ TD) = _7,840_	
Doors	_30_ sqft	(_0.5_ U)(_70_ TD) = _1,050_	(_0.5_ U)(_20_ TD) = _300_
Equipment	_____ watts		(3.4) = _____
	_____ hp		(2500) = _____
Appliances	_____		(_____ sensible) = ↗ _1,200_
Other	_____	_____	(_____ latent) = _____
			residential kitchen

	Subtotals	_77,273_	_33,537_
If ducts are outside the conditioned space add 10%		_(inside)_	_—_
TOTAL BTUH	heat loss	_77,273_	heat gain _33,537_

Check; heat loss = 20-60 BTUH persqft. (south to north); heat gain = 15-60 BTUH per sqft. (north to south). Allow 4% of area served for fan rooms, and 2% of gross building area for central plant equipment.

2.12 OFFICE EXAMPLE, HEAT GAIN CALCULATION

DESIGN CONDITIONS

Maps show a summer dry-bulb temperature of 95°F and a wet-bulb temperature of 76°F (Figures 2.19 and 2.20, location "O"). Desired indoor conditions are 75°F and 50% relative humidity. Time of peak heat gain is estimated as 4 PM. Temperature difference (TD) = 20. Grain difference (GD) = 40 (p. 29). See Figure 2.23 for the example office building plan. Refer to Figure 2.24 for construction details.

PROJECT CONDITIONS

Outdoor air: Select largest of infiltration at 0.5 air changes per hour or ventilation at 15 CFM per person (pp. 13 and 14).

Glass: Double glass U = 0.6. The SC (shading coefficient) for clear double glass is 0.85 (p. 27).

Lighting: Estimate high, 3 watts per sq. ft. of floor area for this office occupancy, and revise as necessary after completing lighting design. Office building lighting installations can range from 1 to 5 watts per sq. ft. depending on luminous intensity, lamp type, and fixture design. (p. 29)

People: 160 occupants seated doing light work.

Ceiling-roof: U = 0.05; weight is 7 pounds per sq. ft.; color is light; ETD = 36 (p. 28).

Walls: U = 0.07; weight is 45 pounds per sq. ft.; color is dark. The west wall is hot at 4 PM; its ETD is 40; the weighted average ETD for all walls at 4 PM is 23 (p. 27).

Doors: U = 1.1 (tempered single glass). Solar gain for doors is included in *Glass*.

Equipment: Allow 1 watt per sq. ft. for electrical equipment operating at the time of peak heat gain. Also allow 10 hp for air handler fans.

QUANTITIES

Outdoor air: Use largest value. Infiltration at 0.5 air changes per hour = 1,980 CFM.

$$(21,600)(11)(0.5) \div 60 = 1,980.$$

Ventilation at 15 CFM per person = 2,400 CFM.

$$(160)(15) = 2,400 \text{ (pp. 13 and 14)}$$

Glass: 1,030 sq. ft. face north (includes 70 sq. ft. of glass door area); 1,440 sq. ft. face south.

Lighting: Totals 64,800 watts at 3 watts per sq. ft.

People: Each occupant produces 250 BTUH sensible plus 150 BTUH latent. (p. 29)

Ceiling-roof: Area is 10,800 sq. ft.

Wall: Net wall area is 10,880 sq. ft.

Doors: Area = 70 sq. ft.

Equipment: Allow 21,600 watts at 1 watt per sq. ft.; plus 10 hp for air handler fans.

SUMMER HEAT GAIN = BTUH

Insert appropriate factors and temperature difference; then complete calculations and total BTUH. Add 10% if ducts are located outside the conditioned zone. Refer back to the heat loss example on page 22 for more detail.

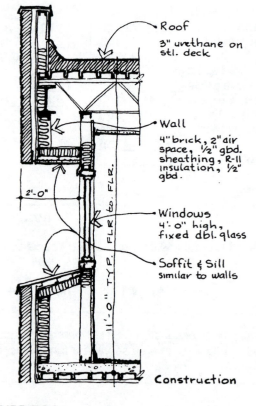

Roof
3" urethane on stl. deck

Wall
4" brick, 2" air space, ½" gbd. sheathing, R-11 insulation, ½" gbd.

2'-0"

11'-0" TYP. FLR. to FLR.

Windows
4'-0" high, fixed dbl. glass

Soffit & Sill
similar to walls

Construction

FIGURE 2.24

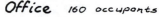

Office   160 occupants

150'

N

60'

210'

Plan

FIGURE 2.23

Office	"O" (map. p.28)	21,600	GJM	1·3·99
project name	location	floor area sqft.	calculated by	date

Design Conditions:

winter

- 70 °Fdb indoor
- 10 °Fdb outdoor
- 60 TD

summer (p. 28)

- 95 °Fdb outdoor
- 75 °Fdb indoor
- 20 TD
- 76 °Fwb outdoor
- 50 % RH indoor
- 40 GD (p.27)
- 4 P.M. time of peak gain

Project Conditions:

Outdoor Air; calculate 1&2 below but use only the **largest CFM** value: ½ A.C.
1. Infiltration based on air change rate 2,970 winter 1,980 summer
2. Ventilation based on CFM per person 2,400 (160@15)

Glass 0.6 U value 0.85 SC (Shading Coefficient)
Lighting 64,800 total watts operating at peak heat gain time
People 160 total occupants at peak heat gain time
Ceiling-Roof 0.05 U value light color 7 weight (lbs/sqft)
Walls 0.07 U value dark color 45 weight (lbs/sqft)
Floor 2 U value, Door ____ U value, Slab Edge U value 0.8
Equipment 21,600 & 10 watts or hp, Appliances —
Other ____

Item	Quantities	Winter Heat Loss = BTUH	Summer Heat Gain = BTUH
Outdoor Air			
winter	2,970 CFM	(1.08)(60 TD) = 192,450	
summer	2,400 CFM		(1.08)(20 TD) = 51,840
			(0.68)(40 GD) = 65,280
Glass total	2,400 sqft	(0.6U)(60TD) = 86,400	(0.6U)(20 TD) = 28,800
N	1,030 sqft ← 960 + 70 doors		(30 SF)(0.85 SC) = 26,265
E	____ sqft		(___ SF)(___ SC) = ____
S	1,440 sqft		(30 SF)(0.85 SC) = 36,720
W	____ sqft		(___ SF)(___ SC) = ____
HOR	____ sqft		(___ SF)(___ SC) = ____
Lighting	64,800 watts		(3.4) = 220,320
People	160 #		(250 sens) = 40,000
			(150 latent) = 24,000
Ceiling-Roof	10,800 sqft	(0.05U)(60TD) = 32,400	(0.05U)(36 ETD) = 19,440
Walls	10,880 sqft	(0.07U)(60TD) = 45,700	(0.07U)(23 ETD) = 17,517
Floor bsmt	____ sqft	(___ factor) = ____	weighted average
slab	10,800 sqft	(2 factor) = 21,600	
crawl space	____ sqft	(___U)(___TD) = ____	
above grade	____ sqft	(___U)(___TD) = ____	
Slab Edge	494 linft	(0.8 U)(60 TD) = 23,700	
Doors	70 sqft	(1.1 U)(60TD) = 4,600	(1.1 U)(20 TD) = 1,540
Equipment	21,600 watts		(3.4) = 73,440
	10 hp		(2500) = 25,000
Appliances	____		(___ sensible) = ____
Other	____		(___ latent) = ____
Subtotals		406,850	630,172
If ducts are outside the conditioned space add 10%		____	____
TOTAL BTUH	heat loss	406,850	heat gain 630,172

Check; heat loss = 20-60 BTUH persqft. (south to north); heat gain = 15-60 BTUH per sqft. (north to south). Allow 4% of area served for fan rooms, and 2% of gross building area for central plant equipment.

REVIEW PROBLEMS

Four kinds of example problems are presented for review purposes. Each problem or group of problems begins with a type key and a page reference; solutions follow each problem.

R and U Values p. 11

1. Find the U value of Wall A shown below.

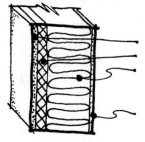

1" stucco
1 1/2" polystyrene
R-19 fiberglass
2×6 softwood studs @ 24" o.c. (not shown)
*1/2" gypsum board

Wall A Section
R Values

Air film outside =	0.2
1" stucco =	0.1
1 1/2" polystyrene @ 4.0 per inch =	6.0
R-19 fiberglass =	19.0
1/2" gypsum board =	0.5
Air film inside =	0.7
R total =	26.5

U = 1/R total = 0.037 = **0.04**

2. If the outdoor temperature is −30°F, and the indoor temperature is 70°F find the temperature of the inside surface of the gypsum board wall. Remember that the temperatures in a construction are proportional to its R values.
   *R from inside air to gypsum board surface is 0.7 and R total for Wall A is 26.5.
   *Temperature difference is 100°F (70 − [−30]).

   Gypsum surface temperature is **67.4°F**
   70 − (100)(0.7)/(26.5) = 67.4

3. The actual cross section of Wall A includes 2×6 softwood studs at 24" centers and 2×6 sill and plate members. Find the U value at a stud.

R Values

Air film outside =	0.2
1" stucco =	0.1
1 1/2" polystyrene =	6.0
5 1/2" softwood =	6.6
2×6 wd. is 1 1/2" × 5 1/2"	
1/2" gypsum board =	0.5
Air film inside =	0.7
R total =	14.1

U = 1/R total **U = 0.07**

4. If 15% of Wall A is made of softwood (studs, sills, and plates) find the exact U value of the wall.

   U 5 0.042 Why is the change so small?
   (15% of 0.07 + 85% of 0.037 = 0.042)

Heat Loss pp. 15–19

5. Find the total heat loss through Wall A during 1 hour on a cold winter night if:
   *the wall area is 1,600 sq. ft.
   *the wall U value is 0.042
   *the outdoor temperature is −20°F
   *the indoor temperature is 68°F

   Heat loss = **5,914 BTUH**
   (1,600)(0.042)(68-{−20}) = 5,914

Heat Gain pp. 24–29

6. Find the total heat gain through Wall A during 1 hour on a hot July day if:
   *the wall area is 1,600 sq. ft.
   *the wall U value is 0.042
   *the outdoor temperature is 100°F
   *the indoor temperature is 78°F
   *the hour is 2 PM (1:30 to 2:30)
   *the wall weighs 20 pounds/sq. ft.
   *the wall faces southwest
   *the stucco is white

   Heat gain = **2,150 BTUH**
   (1,600)(0.042)(32) = 2,150

7. Find an average ETD for Wall A if all the givens from problem 6 are repeated except the wall area is equally divided among four compass orientations (i.e., 25% faces north, 25% faces east, 25% faces south, and 25% faces west).

Average ETD = **24.5°F**

(22+22+32+22)/4 = 24.5

R and U Values p. 11

8. Find a U value for Roof B shown below.

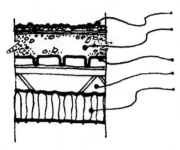

Built-up root 3" lightweight concrete (30 pcf) steel deck-18 ga. 3" air space R-11 fiberglass with foil vapor barrier facing air space? DANGER *see problem* 9 wire mesh support for insulation

Roof B Section
R Values

Air film outside =	0.2
3/8" built-up roof =	0.3
2" lightweight concrete (30 pcf) =	2.0
Steel deck-18 ga. =	0.0
3" air space* =	3.0
R-11 fiberglass with an aluminum foil vapor barrier facing the air space =	11.0
Wire mesh support =	0.0
Air film inside =	0.7
R total	17.2

U = 1/R total = 0.058 = **0.06**

9. If the outdoor temperature is 10°F, and indoor conditions are 70°F dry bulb and 55°F wet bulb, will moisture condense on the aluminum foil vapor barrier in Roof B?

*Begin by finding the temperature of the foil which is proportional to the R value:

R from outside to foil = 5.5, R total = 17.2, temperature difference = 60°F, foil temperature = 29°F

*Then find the dew point temperature of the indoor air on page 0; dew point = 43°F

Since the foil is 29°F and the air dew point is 43°F, moisture **will condense** and ruin the ceiling insulation. Flip the insulation so the vapor faces down and revise the U value calculation in problem 8.

Heat Loss pp. 15–19

10. Find the total heat loss through Roof B during 1 hour on a cold winter night if:
*the roof area is 8,400 sq. ft.
*the roof U value is 0.06
*the outdoor temperature is 0°F
*the indoor temperature is 70°F

Heat loss = **35,280 BTUH**

(8,400)(0.06)(70-0) = 35,280

Heat Gain pp. 24–29

11. Find the total heat gain through Roof B during 1 hour on a hot July day if:
*the roof area is 8,400 sq. ft.
*the roof U value is 0.06
*the hour is 4 PM (3:30 to 4:30)
*the roof weighs 9.6 pounds/sq. ft.
*the roof color is black

Heat gain = **30,240 BTUH**

(8,400)(0.06)(60) = 30,240

Find the heat gain if the roof color is changed from black to white:

Heat gain = **18,144 BTUH**

12. Find the total heat gain through Roof B during 1 hour on a hot July day if all conditions are the same as problem 10 except the roof is flooded with water.

Heat gain = **10,080 BTUH**

(8,400)(0.06)(20) = 10,080

13. A 4-foot square window faces southeast. Find the summer heat gain through the window at 8 AM and at noon if the window is single glass with dark blinds. Outdoor temperature is 95°F and indoor is 75°F. (U value p. 11, SF and SC p. 27)

*An average air space R value has been used in this problem. More precise references would give a lower R value for air spaces in roofs during winter, and a higher R value for air spaces in roofs during summer. Why?

8 AM:
Solar Gain is (SF)(area)(SC)
(160)(16)(70%) =   1,792 BTUH
Conducted gain is (U)(A)(TD)
(1.1)(16)(95-75) =   352 BTUH
                 Heat gain   **2,144 BTUH**
Noon:
Solar gain is (SF)(A)(SC)
(80)(16)(70%) =   896 BTUH
Conducted gain is (U)(A)(TD)
(1.1)(16)(95-75) =   352 BTUH
                 Heat gain   **1,248 BTUH**

Heat Loss and Heat Gain

14. Find the winter heat loss or gain by a 4-foot-square window facing south on a clear January day at noon. Window is single glass with no blind. Outdoor temperature is 10°F, and indoor is 70°F.
Conducted loss is (U)(A)(TD)
(1.1)(16)(70-10) =   −1,056 BTUH
Solar gain is (SF)(A)(SC)
(250)(16)(90%) =   3,600 BTUH
     Net gain   **2,544 BTUH**

15. Same as problem 14 but window faces west.
     Net Loss   **−768 BTUH**

16. Estimate the total solar gain through 1 sq. ft. of single glass during 3 winter months if the glass faces south with no drape. Assume 50% clear days, 50% cloudy days, and a total of 90 days.
Clear days
(45)(1,600)(90%) =   64,800 BTU
Cloudy days (use north value)
(45)(120)(90%) =   4,860 BTU
     Heat gain   **69,660 BTU**

17. Consider the 1 sq. ft. glass area used in problem 16. If the average outdoor temperature is 42°F and the indoor temperature is 70°F, will the glass gain or lose heat during 3 winter months? How much?
Conducted loss is (U)(A)(TD)(90 days)(24 hr)
(1.1)(1)(70-42)(90)(24) =   −66,528 BTU
Solar gain from problem 16 =   69,660 BTU
     Net Gain   **3,132 BTU**

Outdoor Air

18. Find the expected infiltration CFM and ventilation CFM for a 20,000 sq. ft. department store.
*22′ high conditioned space
*built in 1975, no operable windows
*no smoking allowed

Expected infiltration in winter =0.75 air change
(20,000)(22)(0.75)/60 =   **5,500 CFM winter**
                 3,666 CFM summer
Design ventilation all year = 0.2 to 0.3 CFM per sq. ft.—estimate 0.25
(20,000)(0.25) =   **5,000 CFM all year**

19. Find the expected winter peak hourly heat loss due to outdoor air for the department store in problem 18.
*indoor temperature = 72°F
*outdoor temperature = 10°F
*use largest CFM from infiltration or ventilation
(CFM)(1.08)(TD) =   sensible loss
(5,500)(1.08)(72-10) =   **368,280 BTUH**

20. Find the expected summer heat gain due to outdoor air for the department store in problem 18.
*indoor temperature 75°F
*indoor relative humidity 50%
*location: New York City (92°Fdb, 74°Fwb)
*use largest CFM from infiltration or ventilation
*use psychrometric chart
(CFM)(1.08)(GD) =   sensible gain
(5,000)(1.08)(92-75) =   91,800 BTUH
(CFM)(0.68)(TD) =   latent gain
(5,000)(0.68)(97-65) =   108,800 BTUH
     Heat gain   **200,600 BTUH**

21. Find the heat gain due to lighting for a school with a total floor area of 6,000 sq. ft.
Estimate 2 watts per sq. ft.
Heat gain = (watts)(3.4) =   **40,800 BTUH**
(6,000)(2)(3.4) = 40,800

22. Find the heat gain caused by 100 people, standing, doing light work.
Heat gain is (# of people)(BTUH each)
Sensible gain (100)(275) =   27,500 BTUH
Latent gain (100)(475) =   47,500 BTUH
     Heat gain   **75,000 BTUH**
Latent gains are tabulated separately from sensible gains because cooling equipment capacity drops as the latent load decreases.

CHAPTER

3

Heating and Cooling Equipment

*What a splendid day!
no one in all the village
doing anything!*

Shiki

———————

This chapter explains the equipment that produces or moves heat in buildings. Operating cycles are described so that readers can understand the factors that affect heating and cooling efficiency. Strive to accomplish the following four objectives as you read this chapter.

1. Build your knowledge and vocabulary by learning the differences between strip heat and furnaces; absorptive and compressive cooling cycles; and an "air conditioner" and a heat pump.
2. Explain advantages of hydronic heating systems compared to forced-air, and argue in favor of water-air heat distribution in large buildings.
3. Learn that refrigeration and cooling cycles do not create "cool," instead they remove heat from a cool place and discard heat in a warm place.
4. Be able to discuss the significant factors that affect heating and cooling equipment efficiency, and to calculate efficiency consequences of varying SEER and COP ratings.

On completion, check your new skills by completing the review problems at the end of the chapter.

———————

3.0 HEATING EQUIPMENT

Heating equipment may use combustion or electrical energy. Selection is usually an economic decision based on initial and operating cost estimates. The quantity of heat produced by heating equipment is measured in BTU (British thermal units); 1 BTU is defined as the quantity of heat required to increase the temperature of 1 pound of water 1°F.

Boilers, furnaces, and heat pumps are rated in BTUH. They are selected to meet a building's calculated peak heat loss.

COMBUSTION HEATING

Fuels

Natural gas, oil, and coal are all potential fuels for building heating. See Table 3.1. When available, natural gas–fired equipment usually offers the lowest initial cost because fuel storage is not required. Oil-fired systems are more expensive to install because they include a storage tank and a more complicated burner. Coal is the most expensive installation because of storage, handling, and ash disposal requirements. Good operating cost projections should be developed to ensure selection of a heat source and equipment that will provide the lowest life cycle cost.

Furnace or Boiler

Furnaces heat air while boilers heat water. Warm-air furnaces can provide effective heating in smaller buildings where the longest duct run extends less than 100 feet from the furnace. Boilers are preferred for larger projects because hot water carries heat over long distances more economically than warm air. In particular,

water piping requires less building space than duct work, and pumps are more efficient than fans in moving large quantities of heat (see Figures 3.1 and 3.2).

Efficiency

The efficiency of combustion equipment depends on maintaining the correct air-fuel ratio, and on minimizing flue heat losses. Thermal efficiency for well-maintained furnaces or boilers approaches 80%, and "pulse-type" burners which extract heat from flue gasses can reach 95%.

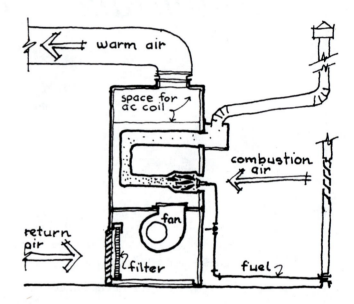

Furnace
FIGURE 3.1

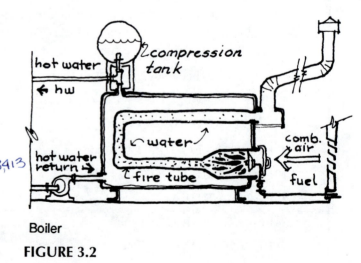

Boiler
FIGURE 3.2

TABLE 3.1

Fuel Heat Content	BTU
Coal (anthracite) per lb	14,000
Electrical per kWh	3,400
Natural gas per MCF	1,000,000
Oil #2 per gallon	140,000
Propane per gallon	90,000
Wood per lb	5,000–7,000

Safety

Safe installations of combustion equipment require:

1. A continuing supply of combustion air to each furnace or boiler (*not* conditioned air from the building).
2. A fire-safe chimney or flue to discharge combustion gasses above the building roof.
3. Limit controls to shut off fuel supply if safe operating temperatures are exceeded.
4. Natural gas supply piping that rises above the ground before entering a building (to prevent underground gas leaks from following the pipe into a building).
5. Vented, fire-resistive chases for gas riser piping in multistory buildings.

ELECTRIC HEATING

Two different types of electric heating are used in buildings. Resistance heaters deliver 3,400 BTU for each kilowatt (kW) of electrical input. Heat pumps deliver more BTUs per kW because they take extra heat from the winter environment.

Resistance (Electric Furnace)

Resistance heating uses electric current to heat Nichrome wire (see Figure 3.3). Familiar small examples include hair dryers and coffee pots. In buildings, resistance heaters are called *strip heat* if they heat air, and *electric boilers* if they heat water. Resistance heating is usually the least expensive equipment to install, and the most expensive to operate. Do not consider resistance heating unless building heating requirements are minimal or electricity costs are especially low.

Heat Pump

A heat pump is a reversible refrigeration machine that takes heat from a cool source and delivers it to a warmer location (see Figure 3.4). Initial cost for a heat pump is higher than strip heat and most combustion heating equipment, but a heat pump can cool a building during summer months.

Electric heat pumps can operate as economically as combustion equipment in mild climates because of the "free" heat they take from the outdoor environment. Like combustion furnaces or boilers, heat pumps can be designed to warm air or heat water de-

pending on the size of the building served. Section 3.5 provides further information about heat pump operation and efficiency.

Efficiency

The efficiency of electric heating is a complex topic. Almost all the electrical energy passing through a building meter is converted to heat by resistance heaters or heat pumps, and each kW of electrical energy yields 3,400 BTU. However, a generating plant that converts fuel energy into electrical energy will consume about 10,000 BTU in fuel for each kW produced. If the efficiency of the generating plant is considered, electric heating would be rated about 33% efficient. However, the extra heat that electric heat pumps take from the environment can make them competitive with combustion heating equipment in mild climates.

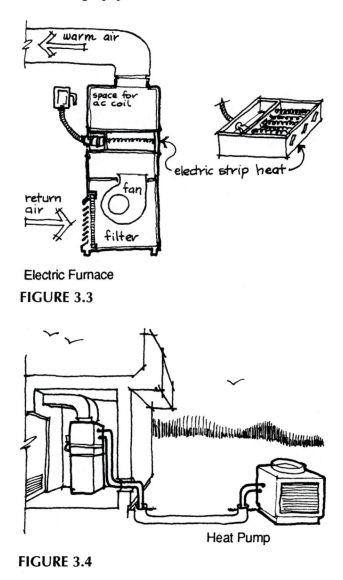

Electric Furnace
FIGURE 3.3

Heat Pump

FIGURE 3.4

3.1 HYDRONIC HEATING

Four components shown in Figure 3.5 comprise a "hydronic" heating installation. Hydronic systems use water as a heat transfer fluid because water can carry BTUs more economically than air. Pumps use less energy than fans, and piping requires less building space than ducts.

Heating system designers choose one of three hydronic heat exchanger types:

- Convectors or radiators
- Radiant surface
- Forced-air

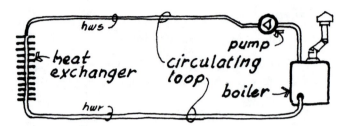

FIGURE 3.5

FIN-TUBE CONVECTORS

Convectors warm room air by contact. Warmed air then rises and is replaced by denser cool air (convective circulation).

Fin-tube convectors are an economical heating choice for homes and are frequently components of HVAC systems in commercial buildings. They are usually located below windows where rising warm air overcomes cold drafts and minimizes condensation. Fin-tube convectors are sometimes called "radiators," but most of their heat transfer is convective (see Figure 3.6).

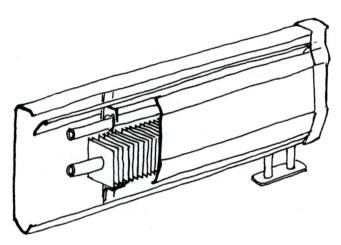

FIGURE 3.6

Construction, Temperature, and Flow

Aluminum fins 2-1/2" square are fitted on 1/2" or 3/4" copper tube. Two water supply temperatures, 140° or 180°F, are used. A protective cover 6 to 8 inches tall is usually attached, but fin-tubes can be built into counters or recessed in the floor below full-height windows. Design water flow through a fin-tube is usually about 1 GPM (gallon per minute).

Fin-tube length for a given BTUH heating load can be estimated using Table 3.2.

Pipe Loops

Figure 3.7 shows *one-pipe* and *reverse return* piping loops used to serve fin-tube convectors. A one-pipe loop is economical, but water temperature drop in the loop means downstream fin-tubes must be longer for a given heat output. A reverse return loop is su-

TABLE 3.2		
BTUH Output per Foot of Fin-Tube		
1 GPM Flow Rate, 65°F Room Air Temperature		
140°F input	1/2" tube	300 BTUH/ft.
180°F input	1/2" tube	550 BTUH/ft.
140°F input	3/4" tube	300 BTUH/ft.
180°F input	3/4" tube	550 BTUH/ft.

Note that tube size has little effect on heating capacity, but the smaller tube increases pump load. Increased flow (GPM) increases BTUH output slightly, but it's not worth the increased pumping cost.

perior to a one-pipe loop because it provides the same water supply temperature at each fin-tube. Constant inlet temperature makes sizing easier and allows better regulation of heat output.

Sizing Examples

Given:

1 GPM flow through 1/2″ fin-tube, 140°F water supply temperature, 65°F room air temperature (at floor).

1. Find the required fin-tube length for a room with a heat loss of 3,600 BTUH.
2. Find the required baseboard radiator length for a room with a heat loss of 1,800 BTUH.
3. Find the panel radiator area needed for a room with a heat loss of 1,800 BTUH.*

PANEL RADIATORS

Panel radiators can replace fin-tubes in rooms where available wall length is limited. They're made from sheet steel or aluminum and are available in a variety of sizes for horizontal or vertical installation. Panel radiators project about 3 inches from the wall surface, but high-output panels have finned backs and may project 6 to 8 inches into the heated space. Typical supply piping is 1/2″ or 3/4″ and heat output per square foot of panel is nearly equal to a fin-tube convector's output per linear foot under similar operating conditions.

BASEBOARD RADIATORS

Extruded aluminum baseboard radiators are a second type of panel radiator (see Figure 3.8). They are smaller than fin-tubes and some find them better looking. Baseboard radiators snap onto wall-

---

*Answers: **1.** 12 feet **2.** 12 feet **3.** 6 sq. ft.

mounted clips. They project about 1 inch from the wall and stand about 5 inches high. Their heat output per foot of length is about half as much as a fin-tube convector, so required length is twice as long for a given heating load.

PUMPS AND ACCESSORIES

Air ejectors are installed to remove air in the piping loop. Air bubbles can damage the pump impeller and impede water circulation.

A compression tank must be installed in the piping loop (see Figure 3.9). It is located to maintain constant water supply pressure at the pump inlet.

Most residential hydronic heating systems circulate less than 10 GPM, and the pump motor is usually less than 1/3 hp. Pumps and GPM for large buildings are discussed on the following pages.

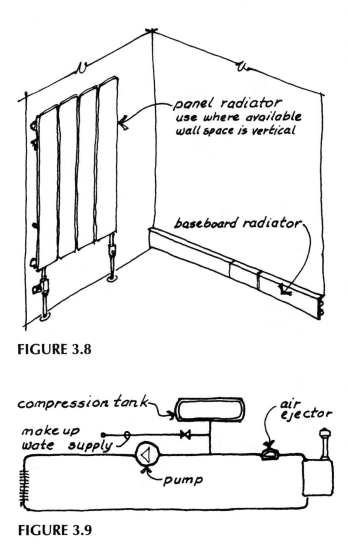

FIGURE 3.8

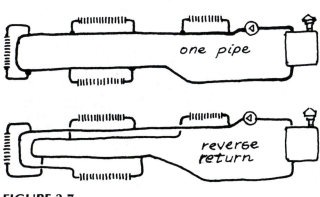

FIGURE 3.7

FIGURE 3.9

3.2 RADIANT HEATING

RADIANT SURFACE

Radiant surface heating is efficient, quiet, invisible, draft-free, and comfortable. The radiating surfaces can be floors, walls, or ceilings, but only floors, warmed by water circulated through embedded piping, are covered here (see Figure 3.10).

Construction

Serpentine pipe loops are embedded in a concrete floor slab, or in lightweight concrete or gypsum poured on insulated floors. Pipe is usually PB (polybutylene) or PEX (polyethylene) plastic tubing in 3/8" to 3/4" sizes, but copper is also used.

Maximum tubing length is 300' for 1/2" tube and 400' for 3/4" tube. Tube spacing varies from 4" to 18", but 12" center to center is fairly typical when heating requirements are not extreme.

Zones, Temperature, and Flow

Serpentine tubing loops form heating zones, and water flow in each zone is adjusted at a distribution manifold. The tube loop serving each zone is positioned so the hottest water flows near exterior walls first.

A mixing valve limits water supply temperature to 110°F, and the design floor surface temperature is 80° to 85°F. Water flow in each zone ranges from 1 to 2 GPM and heating capacity ranges from 25 to 50 BTUH per square foot of floor area.

A disadvantage of radiant floor heating is slow response time. It can take a long time to warm up a cold concrete slab, but once comfortable conditions are established they can be maintained economically.

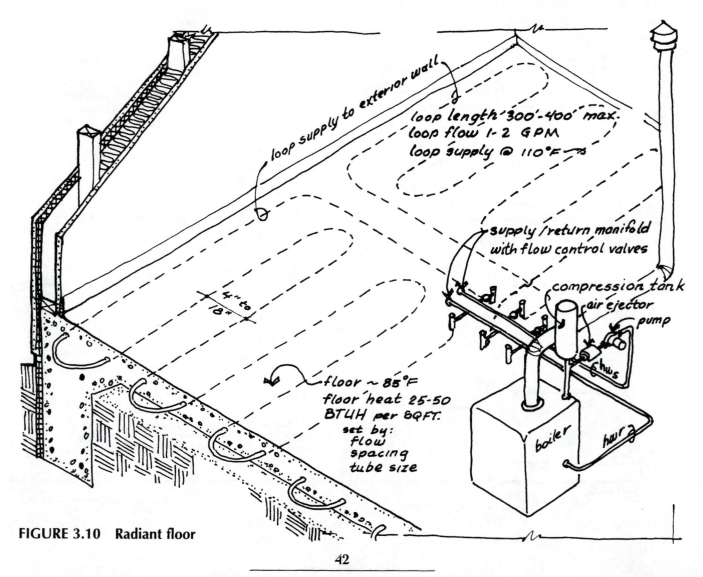

FIGURE 3.10   Radiant floor

3.3 FORCED-AIR HEATING

FORCED-AIR

When a fan is attached to a heat exchanger, the combination can deliver many more BTUH than the convective and radiant equipment illustrated on preceding pages. In residential applications, *central air*, *forced-air*, and *furnace* are appropriate descriptors.

In commercial buildings a heat exchanger–fan combination is called an "air handler" or a "fan coil." Air handlers distribute air to many rooms through a large duct system, while smaller fan coils serve a single room or area without ducts (see Figure 3.11).

Fans increase heat transfer, but they also increase drafts and heating costs. However, air handlers and fan coils are used extensively in commercial buildings, because they can be used for both heating *and* cooling.

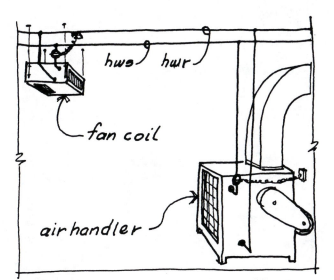

FIGURE 3.11

HYDRONIC GPM, BTUH, AND PIPING SIZES

Water flow and temperature drop across a heat exchanger determine heat output. Flow quantity and velocity set pipe and pump sizes.

Water flow is measured in GPM (gallons per minute) and heating requirements are calculated in BTUH (BTU per hour). In heating applications a 20°F temperature drop across a heat exchanger is usual so 1 GPM will yield about 10,000 BTUH (see Table 3.3).

To estimate forced-air heating GPM for a building or a room, divide the calculated heat loss in BTUH by 10,000. Water velocity in the piping loop is held below 5 feet per second (FPS) to limit pump load. Table 3.4 shows approximate loop piping sizes for various heating loads.

TABLE 3.3

(GPM)(500)(TD) = BTUH

A 1 BTU change will alter the temperature of 1 pound of water 1°F.
1 gallon of water weighs 8.33 lb.
1 GPM = 60 gallons / hour = 500 lb/hour.
TD = temperature difference in °F.
At 20°F TD, 1 GPM yields (1)(500)(20) = 10,000 BTUH.

Note: In radiant floor installations, temperature drop is only 10°F, so 1 GPM yields only 5,000 BTUH.

TABLE 3.4

Heating BTUH (type L copper pipe at 3–5 FPS)

Size	20°TD	GPM
1/2"	30,000	3
3/4"	60,000	6
1"	100,000	10
1-1/4"	160,000	16
1-1/2"	240,000	24
2"	400,000	40
3"	1,000,000	100

3.4 REFRIGERATION CYCLE

Cooling equipment moves heat from cool indoor spaces to warmer outdoor locations (see Figure 3.12). It moves heat by causing a refrigerant to evaporate and condense. Refrigerants capture a lot of heat when they evaporate, and the captured heat is released when refrigerant vapor condenses.

The evaporating or condensing temperature of a refrigerant fluid is dependent on the pressure acting on the fluid. Water evaporates (boils) at sea level pressure at 212°F. However, water on a mountaintop will boil at a lower temperature, and water in a pressure cooker must be raised to a higher temperature before boiling occurs. Water can be used as a refrigerant, but a deep vacuum is required to sufficiently lower its evaporating temperature. Most building cooling equipment uses halocarbon* refrigerant compounds instead of water.

PRESSURE-TEMPERATURE

Cooling equipment maintains a low-pressure *evaporator* and a high-pressure *condenser* in a closed loop of circulating refrigerant. In the low-pressure evaporator, refrigerant boils at 45°F as it takes heat from indoor air. In the high-pressure condenser, hot refrigerant vapor releases heat to outdoor air when it condenses at 125°F.

A *compressor* circulates refrigerant through the loop, and an *expansion valve* maintains low pressure on the suction side of the compressor and high pressure on the discharge side (see Figure 3.13).

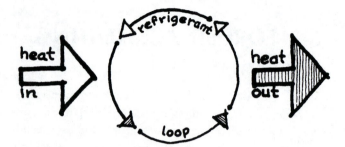

Cooling equipment moves heat

FIGURE 3.12

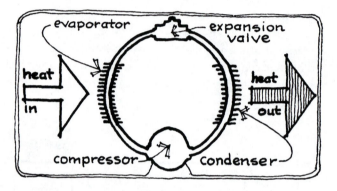

4 cooling cycle components

FIGURE 3.13

FIGURE 3.14

---

*Chlorofluorocarbons (CFCs) were dominant refrigerants from 1931 until the mid-1990s when manufacture stopped to preserve upper atmosphere ozone. Hydrofluorocarbons (HFCs) are slowly replacing CFCs in existing refrigeration equipment. HCFC-22 used in most residential air conditioners and heat pumps is scheduled for 2030 phaseout. Water or ammonia are also used as refrigerants but negative circulating loop pressure (vacuum) is required. See Figure 3.14.

AIR CONDITIONER

The section view in Figure 3.15 shows a window-mounted air conditioner. As the indoor and outdoor temperatures indicate, it moves heat uphill from a cool location to a warm one. An air conditioner's efficiency is a function of indoor/outdoor temperature difference. Greater temperature difference means more input energy and less efficiency, just as driving a car uphill requires more gasoline input and yields fewer miles per gallon. Adding resistance heat strips or using a reversible refrigeration cycle will allow the air condi-

tioner heat or cool. Although just a small window unit is illustrated, the refrigeration cycle components and temperatures are similar in large equipment.

MOVING HEAT

The schematic drawing in Figure 3.16 shows temperatures and pressures within the refrigerant circulating loop. Low pressure on the suction side of the compressor permits the refrigerant to evaporate and capture heat from 75°F indoor air. High pressure on the discharge side of the compressor permits heat release (by refrigerant condensation) to 95°F outdoor air. The schematic shows a window unit, but the cycle is similar for large cooling equipment.

JARGON

A window mounted air-conditioner is called an "air-cooled, DX, packaged unit." DX refers to the direct expansion of refrigerant as a means of cooling indoor air. Larger models of this type of air conditioner are often located on building roofs and connected to duct systems serving several rooms. Rooftop units waste energy when they circulate conditioned air through a poorly insulated outdoor enclosure.

"Split" air conditioning systems avoid energy waste by keeping conditioned air inside the conditioned space. The outdoor section shown in Figure 3.17 is called a condensing unit, the indoor section is an *air handler*, and the connecting refrigerant piping includes liquid and suction lines.

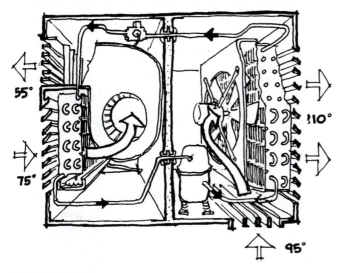

FIGURE 3.15

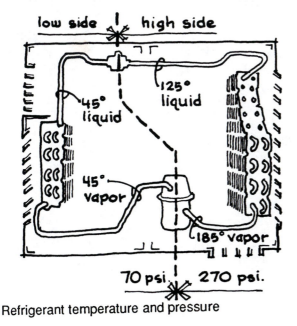

Refrigerant temperature and pressure

FIGURE 3.16

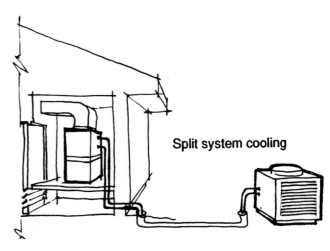

Split system cooling

FIGURE 3.17

AIR CONDITIONING EQUIPMENT

Miles per gallon (mpg) is an index of automobile efficiency. Air conditioner efficiency is measured by a similar index called SEER (seasonal energy efficiency ratio). The SEER rating is an index of an air conditioner's miles per gallon. It is the number of BTUs removed by 1 watt of electrical energy input. Air conditioners are available with SEER ratings that range from 8 to more than 14.

An automobile's mpg changes with load; a car will get less mileage going uphill and more mileage going downhill. An air conditioner's efficiency also depends on load (see Figure 3.18). Cooling load is the difference between heat source and heat sink temperature. Indoor air is the usual heat source, and outdoor air or cooling tower water the usual heat sink. An air conditioner's efficiency can be increased by increasing indoor temperature or by lowering outdoor temperature. Either temperature change means less work for the equipment.

Manufacturers of efficient air-cooled equipment mate small compressors with big condensers. Increased condenser size reduces condensing temperature, cutting compressor load and input energy.

COOLING TOWERS

Water-cooled refrigeration equipment can achieve higher SEER ratings than air-cooled equipment because it is possible to cool water to near the wet-bulb temperature of outdoor air. A cooling tower is an outdoor shower that cools water by evaporation (see Figure 3.19). Cooling towers can cool water 10° to 15°F below ambient air temperature, and this cool water is used to lower condensing temperature and increase SEER. Each ton* of cooling load requires about 3 gallons per minute of cooling tower water, and about 5% of this water is lost to evaporation and drift. River, lake, or well water may offer lower temperatures and higher SEER potential.

---

*A ton is a heat moving rate of 12,000 BTU per hour. Ice plants are rated in tons per day. A ton of water can be converted to a ton of ice by removing 288,000 BTU (12,000 BTU per hour for 24 hours).

105°

85°

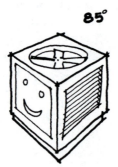

More load = less efficiency

FIGURE 3.18

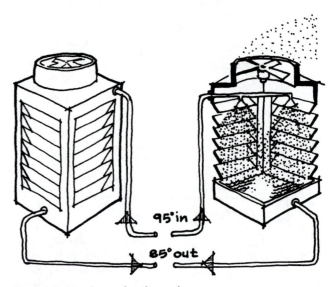

95° in

85° out

Return water is cooler than air

FIGURE 3.19

ABSORPTION

Absorption-cycle cooling equipment uses heat instead of electricity as input energy (see Figure 3.20). A gas flame, hot water, steam, or other heat sources may be used to drive the absorption cycle.

Two components in absorption equipment perform the same jobs as their counterparts in the compressive refrigeration cycle (see Figure 3.21). Refrigerant picks up heat in the *evaporator* and releases heat in the *condenser*. Water can be used as the refrigerant in absorption equipment. An internal vacuum is created allowing water to evaporate at low temperature.

Three absorption-cycle components replace the compressor: in the *absorber* a salt solution absorbs water vapor from the evaporator, a *pump* circulates the diluted salt solution and maintains system pressure difference, and a *generator* boils off water to reconstitute the salt solution.

Efficiency

Unfortunately, absorption-cycle equipment is less efficient than compressive refrigeration. The most efficient absorption equipment uses almost twice as much energy per ton as the best compressive competition. However, absorption equipment may be an excellent choice when waste heat is available from manufacturing processes, electrical generation, or environmental sources.

Absorption machines are large. They can occupy five times as much space as compressive machines of equal capacity (see Figure 3.22).

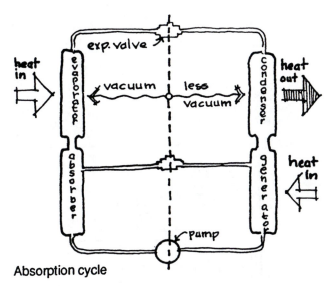

Absorption cycle

FIGURE 3.20

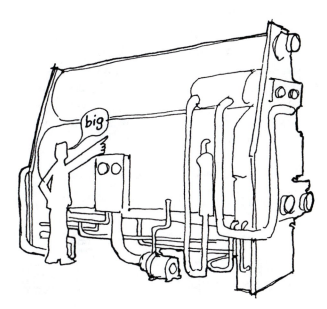

FIGURE 3.22

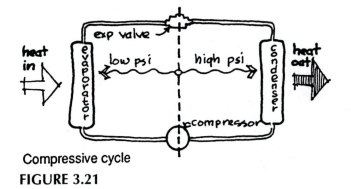

Compressive cycle

FIGURE 3.21

3.5 HEAT PUMPS

A heat pump is a reversible refrigeration cycle machine that can cool or heat. As a cooling unit it takes heat from a building and rejects it to the warm summer environment. As a heater it takes heat from a cool winter environment and delivers it to a building. A four-way reversing valve is used to reverse refrigerant flow, permitting the heat pump to heat or cool (see Figure 3.23).

Like an air conditioner, heat pump efficiency depends on the temperature difference between the environment and indoor air. As the environment gets cooler, a heat pump will deliver less heat.

HEATING EFFICIENCY

The heating efficiency of a heat pump is measured by an index called COP (coefficient of performance). Electric resistance heating devices like strip heaters, toasters, and water heaters, all have a COP of 1. This means they deliver 3,400 BTU from each kilowatt (kW) of electrical energy input. COP ratings of heat pumps range from 1 to more than 4, so heat pumps can deliver much more heat than electric resistance heaters in mild winter climates. A heat pump with a COP of 3 will deliver 10,200 BTU from a 1 kW

input; 3,400 BTU come from the kW, and the additional 6,800 BTU are taken from the winter environment. Winter COP values of 2 or more are possible for air-source heat pumps in cold climates because outdoor air temperatures may be above 20°F for many of the total winter heating hours.

As shown in Figure 3.24, heat pump performance improves with increasing environmental temperature and decreases with decreasing environmental temperature. Therefore, a heat pump produces less heat during cold weather, when it's needed most. To overcome the cold weather output problem, supplemental electric resistance heat is installed to augment heat pump output. Inefficient supplemental resistance heating is operated only when heat pump output is inadequate.

HSPF (heating seasonal performance factor) is a heating efficiency index used instead of COP for residential heat pumps. Like SEER, it is measured in BTU per watt so an HSPF of 6.8 would equal a COP of 2.

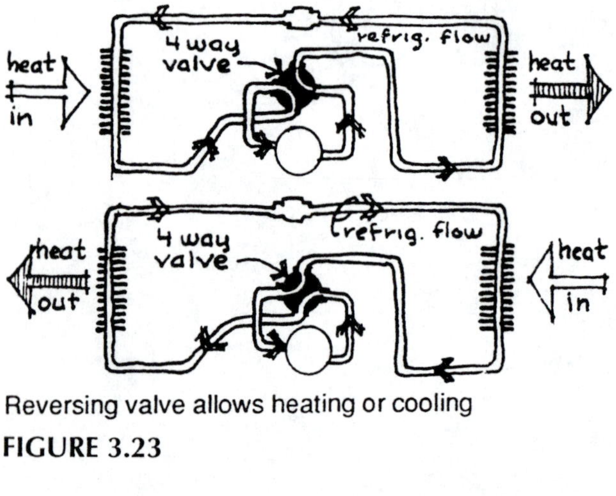

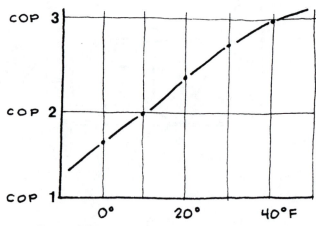

Heat Pump COP changes with source temperature

COP ?
COP 1 = 3,400 BTU per kW
COP 2 = 6,800 BTU per kW
COP 3 = 10,200 BTU per kW

FIGURE 3.24

Reversing valve allows heating or cooling

FIGURE 3.23

AIR-SOURCE HEAT PUMPS

The air-source heat pump shown in Figure 3.25 uses outdoor air as a heat source or heat sink. During cold, damp weather, ice can form on the heat pump's outdoor coil and a defrost cycle is required to permit continuous operation. Supplemental strip heaters must operate when defrosting because the heat pump is taking heat from indoor air to melt ice outdoors.

WATER-SOURCE HEAT PUMPS

Water-source heat pumps use water instead of outside air as a heat source or heat sink. Water from a lake or well is usually warmer than winter air and cooler than summer air, so water-source heat pumps can operate more efficiently than air-source units.

When water is not available the earth may be used as a heat source and sink. A heat pump can be connected to a buried loop of piping which circulates water to give or take heat from the earth. The loop may be vertical like a well or horizontal like a sewer.

The illustration in Figure 3.26 shows an indoor DX air handler, but hydronic heat pumps that produce hot or chill water are available. This hot water could be circulated in a radiant floor-heating installation.

LOOP-CONNECTED HEAT PUMPS

Supermarkets often do all their winter heating with heat rejected by refrigeration equipment. In this ideal situation, refrigeration energy input is used twice. First it cools food, and then it heats the store. Like supermarkets, larger buildings often require heating and cooling at the same time. Heat required at the building perimeter during winter months may be equal to the cooling required at the building's center due to lights and people.

When building heating and cooling loads are balanced, heat pumps connected by a loop of water piping will deliver excellent heating and cooling efficiency (see Figure 3.27).

When heating and cooling loads are out of balance, a boiler and a cooling tower must be used to keep loop water temperature in the range where the heat pumps operate efficiently.

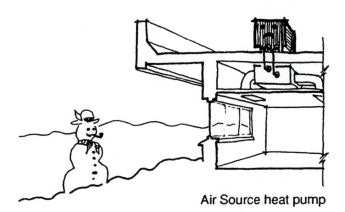

Air Source heat pump

FIGURE 3.25

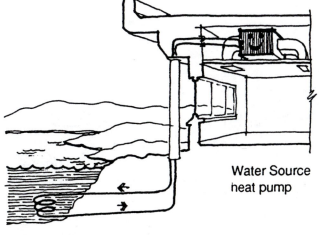

Water Source heat pump

FIGURE 3.26

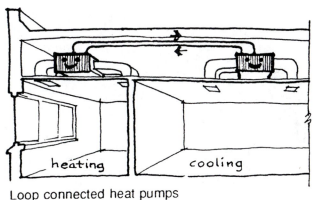

heating   cooling

Loop connected heat pumps

FIGURE 3.27

3.6 LARGE AIR CONDITIONING EQUIPMENT

The schematic in Figure 3.28 shows cooling components of an air-conditioning* installation for a large building.

Component 1 is an *air handler* which mixes fresh and return air, cools and dehumidifies the air mixture, and distributes conditioned air to building spaces. Many air handlers are used in large buildings to achieve comfort control for a variety of building spaces or zones.

Component 2 is called a *chiller.* It includes all parts of the refrigeration cycle described earlier (i.e., evaporator, condenser, compressor, and expansion valve), but instead of cooling air, it chills water which

---

*Air-conditioning is defined as controlling air temperature, humidity, and quality; so heating components should be added to the schematic before describing it as an air-conditioning installation. For the large equipment shown, heating components would typically include boilers, pumps, hot water piping, and heating coils in each air handler.

is pumped to individual air handlers. Using water to carry heat instead of air saves energy and space when transport distances exceed 200 feet.

Component 3 is a *cooling tower* which dumps building heat to the environment by evaporating water. Cooling towers can be more efficient than air-cooled condensers and they require less space.

The sketch in Figure 3.29 shows physical examples of the components in Figure 3.28. Several considerations affect the placement of these components.

1. The **air handler** must have access to fresh and return air. Reserve 4% of the total building floor area to accommodate air handlers.
2. The **chiller** is usually located in the basement because of weight and noise. Allow 2% of the building's gross floor area for chillers, boilers, and electrical equipment. Also provide access for installing and servicing large components.
3. The **cooling tower** is noisy and wet. Select an appropriate outdoor location on the ground or roof. Allow 75 pounds per ton, and 1 sq. ft. per ton for cooling tower weight and size. Creative designers may use fountains or pools to serve as cooling towers.

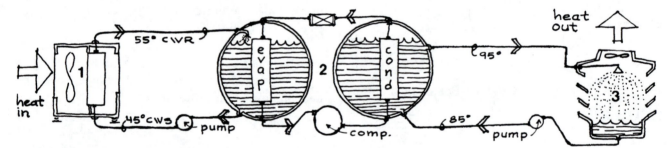

Schematic cooling components

FIGURE 3.28

Physical cooling components

FIGURE 3.29

3.7 HEATING AND COOLING

Air handlers and fan coils can be used for heating *and* cooling when hot and chilled water are circulated throughout a building. Boilers and chillers serve as heat sources or sinks, while air handlers and fan coils add or remove heat from occupied spaces. Moving heat in water instead of air cuts operating costs, so most large buildings use water as an intermediate heat carrier.

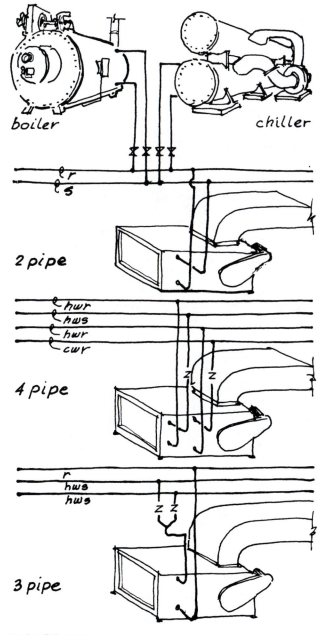

FIGURE 3.30

Three piping arrangements are utilized for heating-cooling applications (see Figure 3.30).

In *two-pipe* installations the heat exchanger in each air handler or fan coil receives hot **or** chill water depending on the season. Two-pipe systems are economical, but changeover to and from heating or cooling is slow. The heat exchangers inside air handlers and fan coils are called "decks" or "coils."

In winter months, large office buildings heat the exterior zones and simultaneously cool the core zone to remove heat from lights and people. *Four-pipe* systems increase piping costs, but they allow coincident heating and cooling and easy and rapid change to and from heating or cooling. Thermostat-controlled valves select hot or chill water, and air handlers often include two heat exchangers appropriately named "hot deck" and "cold deck." (See Figure 3.31.)

Three-pipe installations save some piping dollars by using a common return. Comfort control is as good as a four-pipe system, but when some air handlers are heating and others are cooling, operating costs increase because the return water temperature is high for the chiller and low for the boiler.

AIR VELOCITY AND TEMPERATURE

Design air velocity at the face of the hot deck is usually about 700 FPM (feet per minute), and room air supply temperature varies from 80° to 130°F as controls regulate heat exchanger water flow. Design air velocity at the face of the cold deck is held near 500 FPM to encourage condensation. Room air supply temperature can be as low as 55°F. Refer to Chapter 5 for heating and cooling air quantity calculations and duct sizes.

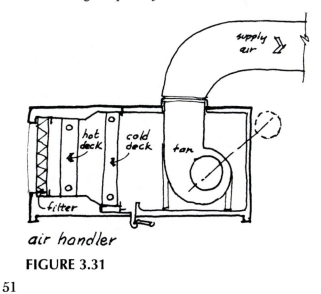

FIGURE 3.31

BOILERS

The drawing in Figure 3.32 illustrates selected parts of a building heating-cooling installation using water as a heat transfer medium.

Calculated building heat loss sets total boiler capacity; oversizing boilers wastes fuel. Because water systems are safer and require less maintenance, most heating boilers deliver hot water instead of steam. Usual water supply temperature is 180°F, but very large heating systems circulate pressurized water at 300°F or more.

Fuel-fired boilers are 80 to 85% efficient at full load, so input for a 100,000 BTUH boiler is about 125,000 BTUH. Most heating boilers operate with a 20°F temperature difference between supply and return so 1 GPM delivers about 10,000 BTUH.

CHILLERS

Calculated building heat gain sets chiller capacity. Many buildings can be served with a single chiller (or boiler), but designers frequently specify three or four smaller units so a mechanical or electrical failure doesn't shut a building down. A typical chiller reduces loop water temperature by 10°F so each GPM circulated in the piping loop will carry about 5,000 BTUH.

Efficient modern chillers consume less than 0.8 kW per ton, but when the total energy required by cooling towers, circulating pumps, and air handlers is added, 3 to 4 kW per ton is not an unusual building HVAC load.

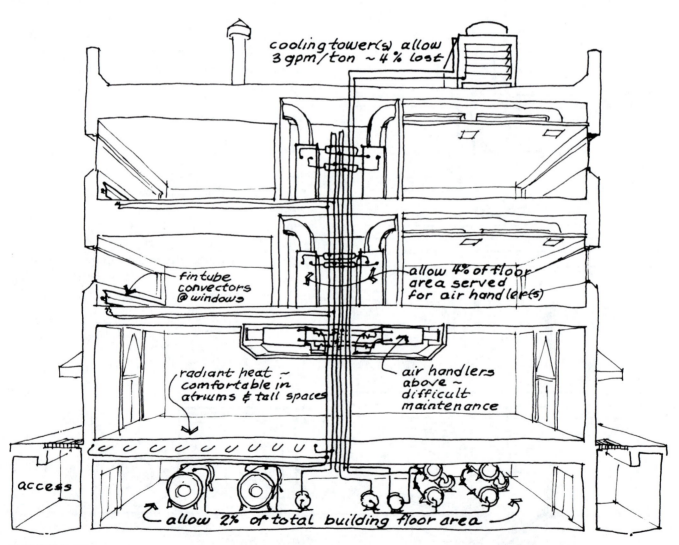

FIGURE 3.32

SPACE REQUIREMENTS

Boilers and chillers are large and heavy so scheduling, delivery, and installation requires careful planning. Combustion air intakes, fire-safe flues, and adequate space for retubing are design and construction considerations.

Remember to allow 4% of the floor area served for air handlers, and allow 2% of total building floor area for boilers, chillers, pumps, and electrical switchgear. Large heavy equipment is usually located in basements or on mechanical floors in tall buildings.

BTUH, GPM, AND PIPE SIZE

The BTUH provided or removed by air handler heat exchangers is determined by the water TD (temperature difference) from inlet to outlet, and water flow in GPM. Many heating installations use a 180°F water supply temperature and design for a 20°F temperature drop across the hot deck. Cooling equipment provides chill water near 45°F and designs for a 10°F gain across the cold deck.

Designers use the chart in Table 3.5 and calculated heating and cooling loads to estimate GPM and pipe size for the entire building or individual air handler zones.

TABLE 3.5

Piping—Heating and Cooling Capacity (field numbers = BTUH)

Pipe Size	Heating 20°TD	Cooling 10°TD	GPM at 3–5 FPS*
1/2"	30,000	15,000	3
3/4"	60,000	30,000	6
1"	100,000	50,000	10
1-1/4"	160,000	80,000	16
1-1/2"	240,000	120,000	24
2"	400,000	200,000	40
3"	1,000,000	500,000	100
4"	2,000,000	1,000,000	200
6"	4,000,000	2,000,000	400
8"	7,000,000	3,500,000	700

*FPS = feet per second, water velocity. Remember to allow for at least 1" thick pipe insulation (more is better); also select hangers and supports that allow pipe movement without insulation damage.

PUMPS

Pump load is measured in "feet of head." A pump lifting water 100 feet is working against 100 feet of head. Head is caused by the weight of water and by friction as water flows through pipe, valves, and fittings. As head increases, pump output drops.

Two factors, GPM and head, must be established before selecting a pump for a particular application. GPM is set to satisfy the heating or cooling load, and head is the total friction in a closed circulating loop. In an open cooling tower, loop head is total friction plus lift.

Pump selection begins after detailing the entire pipe loop and calculating a system curve that illustrates the relationship between flow and head for a particular piping installation. An increase in loop GPM will increase pump head.

Manufacturers provide pump curves that illustrate flow for various heads. Pumps are selected by superimposing pump curves on the system curve to identify a pump that will provide required GPM (see Figure 3.33).

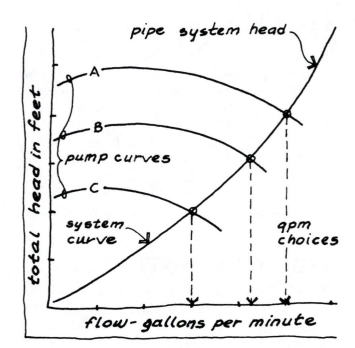

FIGURE 3.33

CONTROLS

A great variety of fittings, temperature sensors, valves, and control devices are not covered in this text. Owners seeking the best available HVAC equipment understand an installation is only as good as its controls.

REVIEW PROBLEMS

1. Select oil or natural gas heating, choosing the most economical heating fuel based on the following:
   - #2 fuel oil sells for $0.80 per gallon and a 75% efficient oil furnace is available.
   - Natural gas sells for $6.80 per MCF and an 80% efficient furnace is available.
2. If electricity sells for $0.07 per kW how much more expensive is electric resistance heating compared to oil heat from problem 1?
3. A home has a peak heat loss of 25,000 BTUH. Estimate the total length of fin-tube convector needed to heat the home with 180°F water.
4. A 1,200 sq. ft. home with a peak heat loss of 24,000 BTUH will use hydronic radiant floor heating. Estimate total heating GPM.
5. Name the four refrigeration cycle components.
6. Which components absorb or reject heat?
7. A 4-ton, air-cooled, DX cooling unit has a SEER of 8. If the unit operates 1,200 hours during a typical summer how many kWh (kilowatt hours) of electrical energy will it consume?
8. If a SEER 12 unit replaces the 4-ton cooling unit in problem 7, what will be the annual % savings in electrical consumption?
9. The cooling tower for a 200-ton chiller will weigh about ___ pounds and circulate about ____ GPM.

10. If an electric heat pump operates with an average annual COP of 2.8 find the number of BTU it will deliver for $1.00. Assume $0.07 per kWh.

11. How much space should be allowed for air handlers and heating-cooling equipment in a 50,000 sq. ft. building?

After completing problems 1 through 11 you should be able to set up and solve this last problem before looking at the answer. Use the following heating-cooling loads, costs, annual operating hours, and efficiencies:

- oil cost is $0.78 per gallon
- electricity cost is $0.08 per kWh
- annual heating hours = 2,000
- annual cooling hours = 800
- building peak heat loss is 600,000 BTUH
- building peak heat gain is 400,000 BTUH
- boiler efficiency is 80%
- chiller SEER is 9
- heat pump SEER is 10
- heat pump COP is 2.3

12. A school board is considering two options for heating and cooling a new high school. Option A will use an oil-fired boiler for heating and an electric chiller for cooling. Option B will use electric heat pumps for heating and cooling. Find the annual heating-cooling cost for each option and select the option that will provide the lowest cost.

ANSWERS

1. Oil will be about 12% cheaper.
2. Electric resistance costs about 270% more.
3. 45 feet total
4. 5 GPM
5. compressor, condenser, evaporator, and expansion valve
6. Evaporator absorbs, condenser rejects.
7. 7,200 kWh
8. 33% savings (2,400 kWh less)
9. 15,000, 600
10. 136,000 BTU per $1
11. 2,000 sq. ft. for air handlers and 1,000 sq. ft. for heating-cooling equipment
12. Begin by finding the total annual BTU required for heating and cooling.

Heating:
$$(600,000)(2,000) = 1,200,000,000 \text{ BTU}$$

Cooling:
$$(400,000)(800) = 320,000,000 \text{ BTU}$$

Next find the heating cost with oil and heat pumps:

Oil heat cost per year = $8,357
$$(1,200,000,000)(\$0.78) \div (140,000)(80\%)$$

Heat pumps cost per year = $12,276
$$(1,200,000,000)(\$0.08) \div (3,400)(2.3)$$

Next find the cooling cost with chiller and heat pumps:

Chiller cost per year = $2,844
$$(320,000,000)(\$0.08) \div (9)(1,000^*)$$

Heat pumps cost per year = $2,560
$$(320,000,000)(\$0.08) \div (10)(1,000^*)$$
$$^*1,000 \text{ watts per kW}$$

Annual heating-cooling cost: Option A = $11,201
Annual heating-cooling cost: Option B = $14,836

Select Option A
Other factors that should be considered in the heating-cooling equipment selection process include initial costs, anticipated maintenance costs, and related energy costs for fans and pumps. Chillers are very efficient heat movers, but pumps and cooling tower fans cut their system SEER.

CHAPTER

4

Building Air-Conditioning

*My two plum trees are
so gracious . . . see they flower
one now, one later.*

Buson

———◦———

This chapter builds on completed readings about heating-cooling equipment operation and efficiency. New information about air distribution is presented, and case studies are used to illustrate building applications. On completion you should be able to select air-conditioning equipment for a particular building project.

The chapter begins with a discussion of the components used to distribute conditioned air to individual rooms or zones in a building. Study four zoning alternatives that HVAC system designers consider for specific buildings to understand their comparative advantages and limitations. Also learn the difference between constant volume (CV) and variable air volume (VAV) air-conditioning systems. Some buildings are easily conditioned with one equipment type or configuration but others require several.

Selecting air-conditioning equipment is an activity that seeks maximum quality at minimum cost. Unfortunately, increased quality usually increases *first* cost, but experienced system designers know that the benefits of a quality installation are found in improved comfort and reduced *operating* costs.

Case studies demonstrate the equipment selection process, and the residence and office examples developed in Chapter 2 are used to explore alternatives in selecting and zoning air-conditioning installations.

When you are comfortable with the material covered, complete the review problems at the end of the chapter.

———◦———

4.0 AIR-CONDITIONING— ZONING

COMPONENTS

Most air-conditioning installations use the following five components to control and distribute conditioned air in buildings (see Figure 4.1):

1. An *air handler* that controls air quantity, temperature, humidity, and quality as it filters and circulates air
2. A *supply duct* system that distributes conditioned air to each outlet in the building
3. A *return* path that carries air back to the air handler (may be ducted or an open plenum)
4. Provision for *exhaust* air to minimize odors and airborne contaminants (usually exhausted at kitchens, laboratories, and rest rooms)
5. A *fresh air* intake to maintain indoor air quality.

Components 3, 4, and 5 are not shown on the following pages for simplicity, but they will be included in all quality air-conditioning installations.

ZONING ALTERNATIVES

At any given time different rooms in a building may have different requirements for heating or cooling. On a winter day a lobby with large windows needs lots of heat, but an interior auditorium filled with people will need much less heat or perhaps cooling. HVAC system designers select from four zoning alternatives to distribute conditioned air in buildings.

1. **Individual units** separately heat or cool each room in a building.
2. **Single-zone** installations heat or cool all building rooms with a single conditioned air supply.
3. **Zoned** installations subdivide a building into zones and deliver discrete conditioned air supplies to each zone. A zone is a group of rooms with similar heating-cooling requirements.
4. **Multizone** installations heat or cool rooms (zones) by providing a discrete conditioned air supply to each room (zone).

The following discussion describes each zoning alternative. Very large buildings may use several equipment types and zoning schemes to satisfy a variety of heating and cooling requirements.

Type 1: Individual Units

Individual units are available for through-wall or in-room mounting (see Figure 4.2). They are an excellent choice for conditioning spaces like hotel guest rooms because they permit individual temperature control and prevent transfer of smoke or odors from one room to another. Two types of individual units are available:

Individual Unit
FIGURE 4.2

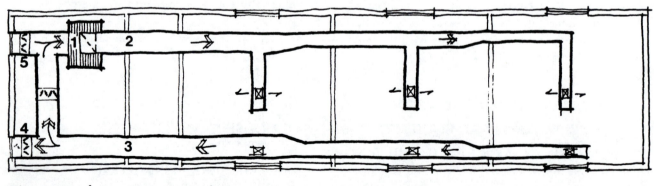

Plan - zoning components
FIGURE 4.1

1. *Fan coils* use hot or chilled water as a heat source or heat sink so boilers and chillers are required to serve them. Fan coils served with a two-pipe distribution system can heat or cool, but not at the same time. Four-pipe hot and chill water distribution is more adaptable because it permits some fan coils to deliver heat while others cool.

2. *Packaged units* contain heat-producing and heat-moving equipment. Examples include heat pumps and air conditioners with strip heat. Loop-connected heat pumps that use water circulating in a closed piping loop as a heat source or sink, can be very efficient in buildings with simultaneous heating and cooling requirements.

Type 2: Single Zone

Single-zone installations are a good choice for conditioning a large room or a group of similar rooms (a zone). A single-zone system could be used for a building with a single row of identical adjoining rooms (see Figure 4.3). If each room has the same number of occupants, the same lighting, and the same window area and orientation, room air-conditioning requirements will be very similar, and a single-zone installation can provide and maintain comfortable conditions.

Type 3: Zoned

Consider a school where half the classrooms face south and the other half face north. On a sunny winter day, the southern classrooms will enjoy substantial solar heat gain and therefore need less heat than the northern classrooms. A single-zone installation cannot provide optimum comfort for all classrooms because it delivers only a single air temperature.

Two single-zone air handlers, one serving southern classrooms and the other serving northern class-

rooms, can maintain comfortable conditions in all classrooms. When more than one single-zone air handler is used, a HVAC installation is described as "zoned" (see Figure 4.4).

Type 4: Multizone

Multizone equipment can provide excellent temperature control for buildings with a variety of air-conditioning requirements. A multizone installation can deliver warm air to one room or zone and, at the same time, provide cool air to an adjacent room or zone. Three types of multizone equipment are used in building applications: reheat, double duct, and individual duct.

Multizone reheat installations deliver cooled air to reheat terminals where a thermostat controls the supply air temperature for each room or zone (see Figures 4.5 and 4.8). Reheat equipment can provide excellent temperature and humidity control, but it wastes energy and is expensive to operate because the user pays twice (first to cool and then again to reheat).

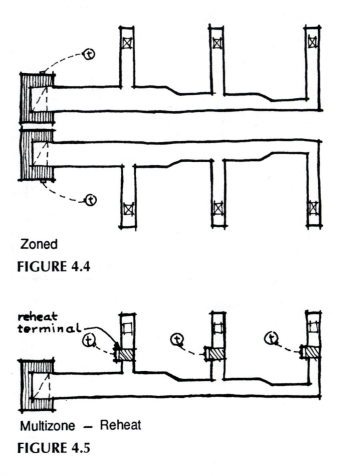

Zoned
FIGURE 4.4

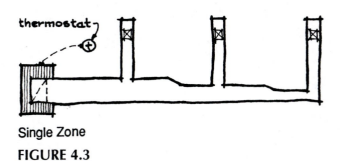

Single Zone
FIGURE 4.3

Multizone — Reheat
FIGURE 4.5

Multizone double duct installations include separate warm and cool air ducts throughout the building. These ducts deliver conditioned air to "mixing boxes" where a thermostat adjusts inlet dampers to control air temperature (see Figures 4.6 and 4.8). Double duct equipment can provide excellent temperature control, but double duct systems often operate in a mixing mode which wastes energy (they mix cool and warm air to control zone temperature).

Multizone individual duct installations include separate ducts from an air handler to each conditioned room or zone (see Figure 4.7). Thermostats control dampers in the air handler which proportion a mixture of warm and cool air for each zone served. Individual duct equipment is available in mixing or bypass configurations (see Figure 4.9).

The mixing type is essentially the same as a double duct installation except mixing occurs in a central air handler instead of remote mixing boxes. The bypass type does not mix warm and cool air; instead it blends warm or cool air with return air. Bypass installations offer good temperature control without the energy waste typical of mixing installations.

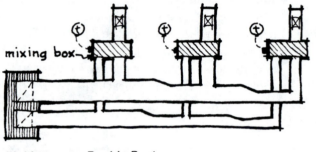

Multizone — Double Duct

FIGURE 4.6

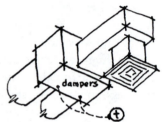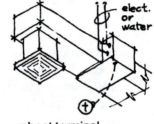

mixing box   reheat terminal

FIGURE 4.8

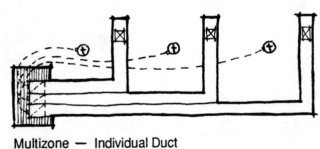

Multizone — Individual Duct

FIGURE 4.7

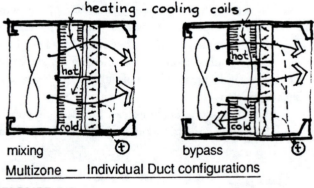

Multizone — Individual Duct configurations

FIGURE 4.9

CV OR VAV AIR SUPPLY?

Most of the preceding zoning alternatives can be equipped with CV (constant volume) or VAV (variable air volume) fans. In CV installations the temperature of conditioned air is changed to satisfy heating or cooling loads, and a constant quantity of air is provided as long as the fan operates. With VAV installations, fan output is controlled so that the quantity of conditioned air varies in response to changing heating or cooling loads.

VAV installations use less fan energy than constant volume equipment, and fan energy can be a substantial part of total energy consumption in sealed buildings where fans may operate 8,760 hours each year. VAV equipment is specified to reduce annual energy costs. Reduced conditioned air quantity saves energy, but it can cause comfort problems including inadequate room air circulation and loss of humidity control.

A VAV installation looks similar to a constant volume system except for a variable output fan and a VAV box or terminal which modulates the amount of air delivered to each space or zone (see Figure 4.10).

Two refinements have been developed to overcome the inadequate room air circulation problem typical of VAV installations operating with reduced air output. VAV induction terminals or VAV fan-powered terminals recirculate room air as the ducted air supply is cut back (see Figure 4.11). Unfortunately both of these terminals increase system fan energy requirements.

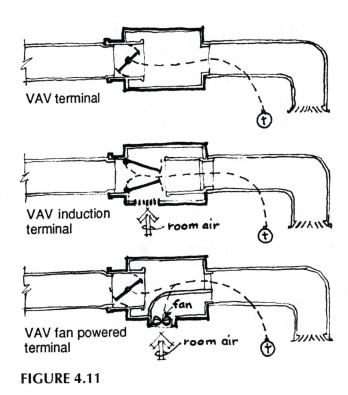

FIGURE 4.11

SUMMARY

Individual units offer the lowest first cost for conditioning many small spaces. Single-zone equipment can offer low first cost for a large space or a group of similar spaces. Both individual units and single-zone installations can be operated economically when quality equipment is specified.

Zoned and multizone equipment can offer better temperature control than individual units or single-zone equipment. It is also more expensive to install and operate (except multizone individual duct bypass which can be operated as economically as single-zone equipment).

VAV installations can cut fan energy compared to constant volume equipment. However, reduced air movement and poor humidity control are potential VAV comfort problems that require careful zoning and a precise analysis of building heating-cooling load variations.

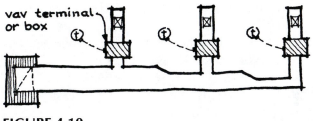

FIGURE 4.10

4.1 SELECTING HVAC EQUIPMENT

Performance requirements are the appropriate starting point for HVAC equipment selection. In a hospital, excellent temperature control is important. In a rare-book library, humidity control can be critical. In a recording studio the allowable background noise level is a significant air-conditioning performance consideration. Designers selecting equipment for a specific building try to maximize performance and minimize cost. The selection process involves many variables, but four decision areas are essential considerations:

1. Heating
2. Cooling
3. Zoning
4. Efficiency

HEATING CONSIDERATIONS

Equipment alternatives for heating systems include furnaces, boilers, and heat pumps. Use a furnace in smaller buildings when warm air is to be delivered to rooms less than 100 feet away from the furnace. Choose a boiler for large buildings where heat must be delivered over long distances.

Select combustion equipment when fuel is available at a good price compared to electrical energy. Where electrical energy is economical and winters are mild, use heat pumps to deliver warm air in small buildings or hot water in large buildings.

COOLING CONSIDERATIONS

Equipment choices for cooling systems include air conditioners, heat pumps, or chillers. Use chillers in large buildings where cooling is provided by many air handlers (absorption chillers may be economical if waste heat is available).

All cooling equipment must reject heat into the environment. Air-cooled condensing units or heat pumps reject heat from smaller DX equipment because they are easy to install and maintain. For larger air-conditioning installations (over 50 tons) consider cooling towers or evaporative condensers to reject heat because they require less space than air-cooled

equipment and can offer improved efficiency. If lake or well water is available, it can replace a cooling tower and improve efficiency.

ZONING CONSIDERATIONS

Equipment choices for zoning include individual units, single-zone, or multizone equipment. Selection is based on operating requirements for each particular building.

EFFICIENCY CONSIDERATIONS

Designers who choose to save energy at every opportunity can produce efficient and excessively expensive buildings. It is not productive to invest in every possible energy-conserving opportunity because each added investment will return smaller energy savings.* Efficiency considerations must include specific building details. A new efficient air-conditioning system will save *less* energy in a well-insulated building than in an equal but poorly insulated structure.

The following checklist offers possible efficient equipment options.

1. Efficient furnace or boiler (up to 95%)
2. Efficient cooling equipment (SEER 12+)
3. Evaporative cooling in dry climates
4. Absorption equipment run on waste heat
5. Efficient heat pumps (COP 3 to 4, and a SEER of 12+)
6. Use of well water, lake water, or the earth as a heat source and heat sink
7. Heat recovery units to recycle heat from condensers, cooking, manufacturing, or from building exhaust air
8. Economizer equipment—dampers and controls that substitute outdoor air for cooling equipment when weather permits
9. On-site electrical generation with waste heat used for building heating and cooling
10. Use of variable volume air distribution to reduce fan energy

---

*Chapter 6 of this text (Annual Costs) evaluates energy-conserving alternatives in terms of the first year's rate of return on investment.

4.2 CASE STUDY 1: RETAIL BUILDING

"Discount Dan's" (see Figure 4.12) is a national chain retailer with a standard store plan (not a design award winner, but prices are low and profits are good). The store interior is one large space. Dan's construction managers want a HVAC installation with these characteristics:

- Low initial cost
- Low operating cost
- Minimal equipment maintenance
- HVAC failure should not close the store

HEATING SELECTION

Select gas heat or heat pumps depending on the local climate and gas versus electric costs. Specify several small units instead of a single large one to permit continuing store operation should one unit fail. Contract for maintenance with a local HVAC firm that stocks replacement parts.

COOLING SELECTION

Select DX air-cooled condensing units when gas heating is chosen (note: building codes prohibit gas furnaces in plenums).

Heat pumps and gas-electric units are available in single-package or split-system configurations (see Figures 4.13 and 4.14). Single-package units are easy to install but split-system units are more efficient. Long refrigerant piping runs are not desirable so locate split-system outdoor units near their indoor air handlers.

Outdoor equipment is noisy. Screen it from frequently used people areas or put it on the building roof. Rooftop equipment increases roof loads and service access is difficult, but ground space is valued for parking and building access.

ZONING

Select single-zone, constant volume equipment. A multizone installation is more expensive, and its ability to heat and cool at the same time is not required for the large retail space. Variable volume equipment might save some energy, but temperature set back when the store is closed will cost less and save more.

The hung ceiling conceals equipment and ducts, and creates a plenum return path to the air handlers. Fresh air intakes are built into single-package units, but a duct is required for split-system equipment.

EFFICIENCY

Decisions about furnace efficiency, heat pump COP, and air-conditioning SEER will be based on a rate of return analysis for the more expensive high-efficiency equipment. Fan energy can be conserved by night temperature set back when the store is closed.

Comment: Single-package rooftop units are popular for stores like Dan's (a single-package unit includes heating, cooling, and air handling in one enclosure). Single-package equipment is a bit more expensive than split-system equipment but installation is simpler. Split-systems are more efficient because they keep conditioned air inside the building instead of circulating it through a poorly insulated outdoor enclosure.

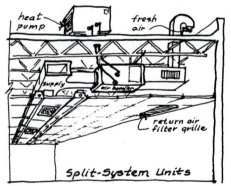

FIGURE 4.13

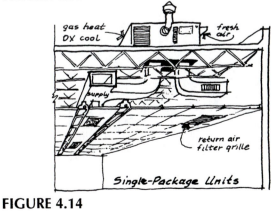

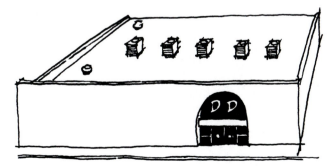

FIGURE 4.12

FIGURE 4.14

4.3 CASE STUDY 2: OFFICE TOWER

This elegant office tower is a tribute to a persuasive developer, a flush banker, a lucky architect, and a capable contractor. A glass salesman is a happier and richer person because of this tower (see Figure 4.15).

The developer's priorities for HVAC were as follows:

* Very good comfort control
* Low operating cost
* Low initial cost

HEATING SELECTION

Select boilers because of building size. If gas or oil is not available compare electric boilers with water-source heat pumps. Circulate hot water to air handlers throughout the building to meet heating requirements. Specify several boilers so that an equipment failure will not shut down the entire building in cold weather.

COOLING SELECTION

Select chillers and circulate chill water to air handlers throughout the building to satisfy cooling loads. Several chillers will be specified to provide partial capacity in the event of an equipment failure. Choose cooling towers to reject waste heat. Locate them at or near ground level if space is available. Otherwise, put them on the building roof.

ZONING

Divide each building floor into an interior *core zone* and exterior *skin zones* (see Figure 4.16).

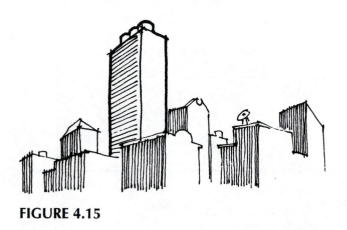

FIGURE 4.15

Select a single-zone, VAV air handler for the core zone on each floor. The building's core will need constant cooling because of internal heat from people and lights, and cutting fan output on nights and weekends will save energy. Select zoned, constant volume equipment to handle the building's skin loads. Provide a separate zone for each orientation to control skin heat gains and losses (see Figure 4.17). Deliver conditioned air below windows in cold climates or at the ceiling in warm climates.

EFFICIENCY

VAV air handlers will save energy and operating dollars on nights and weekends when the core is unoccupied. Specify heat recovery equipment that recycles heat from exhaust air, and economizer cycle controls that use outdoor air for core zone cooling during winter months.

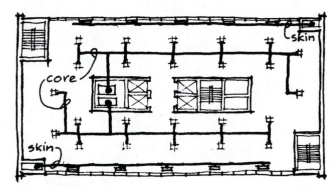

Typical Floor Zoning

FIGURE 4.16

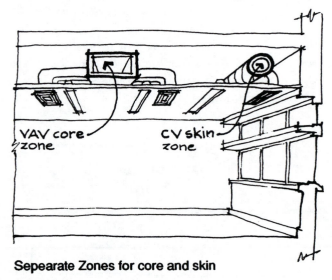

Sepearate Zones for core and skin

FIGURE 4.17

4.4 CASE STUDY 3: CHURCH

The First Savior Church is planning a new sanctuary in a small southern town (see Figure 4.18). The church serves 600 members. Two services are conducted on Sunday morning, and a third is scheduled for Wednesday evening.

The congregation's HVAC requirements are:

- Low initial cost
- Low operating cost

HEATING SELECTION

Select a gas or oil furnace if reasonably priced fuel is available. The church will not be heated during unoccupied hours, so oversize the furnace to permit rapid building warm-up on a cold Sunday morning. If gas or oil is not available a small heat pump could be used to store heat during the week.

COOLING SELECTION

Select ice tank equipment for cooling (see Figure 4.19). It consists of a small refrigeration unit that produces ice in an insulated storage tank. When church cooling is required, the air handler uses chill water circulated through a heat exchanger in the ice storage tank.

Ice tank equipment is appropriate because the church requires a lot of cooling capacity for a short time. Electrical energy costs include a charge for peak demand, and large air-conditioning equipment demands a lot of electrical energy. Peak demand charges can account for most of a church's monthly electric bill. The ice tank lets a church have 20 tons of cooling capacity on Sunday morning without the peak demand (and electric bill) of a 20-ton air conditioner. Savings on peak charges can pay the extra cost of an ice tank installation in many utility service areas.

ZONING

A single-zone, constant volume air handler is the appropriate choice for church heating and cooling. More expensive multizone equipment that can heat and cool at the same time is not needed in a single large interior space like a church.

EFFICIENCY

Efficiency considerations for a church like First Savior are very different from decisions for buildings with continuous occupancy. The church saves energy by limiting peak electrical demand and by turning HVAC equipment off during unoccupied hours instead of investing in added insulation.

FIGURE 4.18

FIGURE 4.19

4.5 CASE STUDY 4: HOTEL

Heart Hotel is a 500-room downtown facility with plush meeting and dining facilities (see Figure 4.20). Design features include a large atrium that delights the eye with twinkling elevators, and pedestrian activity.

The hotel's HVAC requirements include:

- Individual temperature control for guest rooms
- Acoustical privacy for guest rooms
- Quick repairs for guest room equipment
- Individual temperature control for meeting and dining rooms with a variety of occupancy levels
- Low operating cost
- Heat for the atrium in winter

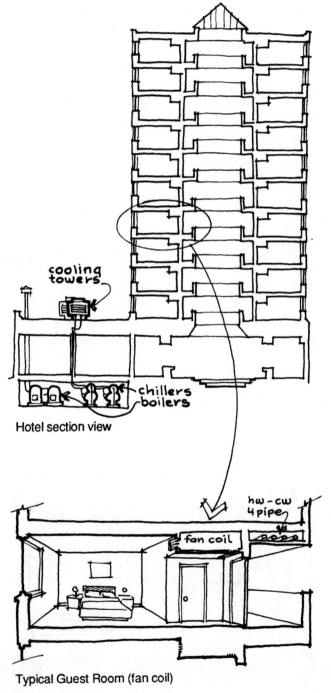

cooling towers

chillers
boilers

Hotel section view

Typical Guest Room (fan coil)

hw – cw
4 pipe

fan coil

FIGURE 4.20

HEATING SELECTION

Select boilers for heating a building of this size and complexity. Hot water supply and return piping requires much less space than duct work and will help to minimize building height. Hot water will be piped to fan coils in each guest room and to single-zone air handlers serving each dining or meeting room. Heat the atrium using a radiant floor warmed by embedded hot water piping. Warm air heating will not work in the atrium because convection causes warm air to rise above the occupied area.

COOLING SELECTION

Select chillers to cool a building of this size. Circulating chilled (and hot) water throughout the building permits each fan coil or air handler to cool or heat as required by room occupants. Specify a four-pipe system instead of three-pipe to avoid mixing chill and hot water in a common return. Select cooling towers to reject waste heat because they offer less size and more efficiency than air-cooled condensing units.

ZONING

Specify a fan coil in each guest room to provide individual control and to ensure acoustical privacy. Detail fan coils for quick replacement in event of failure and keep spares available in the hotel's maintenance department.

In meeting and dining rooms there are two viable zoning options: select single-zone constant volume air handlers for each room, or choose single-zone VAV air handlers that can conserve fan energy when meeting or dining room occupancy is low. Remember two or more single-zone air handlers can be described as a "zoned" installation, but not as multizone equipment.

EFFICIENCY

Quality hotels select quality equipment and operate it only when conditioned spaces are occupied. They also invest in heat exchangers to recycle waste heat from laundries and kitchens to minimize winter heating costs.

Comment: Individual (through the wall) heat pumps or AC units with strip heat could be used instead of fan coils in guest rooms. These units are popular in motels where their noisy operation is used to mask outdoor sounds and the next room's TV, but quiet units are available for hotel applications.

HEART HOTEL: A MORE EFFICIENT WAY?

The four-pipe boiler/chiller installation with fan coils was typical for large hotels built before 1980. However, loop-connected water-source sink heat pumps

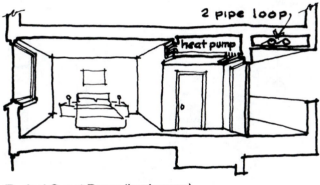

Typical Guest Room (heat pump)

FIGURE 4.21

are specified in many new hotels because they can reduce operating costs (see Figure 4.21).

Physically installations of four-pipe fan coils and loop-heat pumps are quite similar. Both employ a boiler and cooling tower, and both use water to carry heat. The big advantage of loop-heat pumps is that they are very efficient when heating and cooling are required simultaneously (i.e., when guest rooms require heating at the same time meeting rooms or dining areas require cooling because of people and lighting loads). A four-pipe system must operate boilers and chillers all year, but when heating and cooling loads are balanced, loop-heat pumps can heat and cool—without running boilers, or cooling towers.

Initial cost of a loop-heat pump system is competitive with a four-pipe installation, and loop connected heat pumps can provide substantial savings in operating costs. When building heating and cooling requirements are nearly equal, the loop's boiler and cooling tower need not operate. The heat pumps just shift heat between rooms. When heating is required, the boiler is used to maintain 50° to 60°F loop temperatures. This ensures a high COP for the heat pumps, good boiler efficiency, and minimal heat losses from system piping. When cooling is required a cooling tower maintains loop temperatures in the 85°F range to ensure a high SEER for the heat pumps (see Figure 4.22).

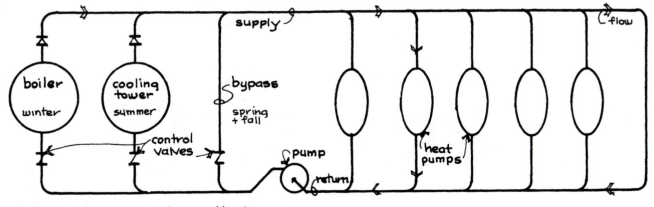

Schematic diagram - water loop and heat pumps

FIGURE 4.22

4.6 HOUSE EXAMPLE, HVAC OPTIONS

Many different HVAC systems could be used to condition the example house from Chapter 2 (see Figure 4.23). This summary discusses four options with increasing initial cost and performance capabilities.

OPTION 1: CONVECTORS

Convectors can provide low-cost temperature control in climates where just heating and ventilation are sufficient for year-round comfort. The installation includes a boiler, a piping loop, and convectors located below windows. Convective air circulation distributes heat within individual rooms.

A single-pipe loop offers lowest initial cost, but it tends to deliver more heat to rooms near the boiler. A two-pipe reverse return installation will provide better heat distribution for a small increase in first cost (see Figure 4.24). Boiler fuel is selected based on local availability. The boiler can also provide domestic hot water, so a separate water heater is not required.

OPTION 2: INDIVIDUAL UNITS

Individual heat pumps or air conditioners with strip heat can provide comfortable indoor conditions. They would be installed below windows of each room. Individual units can provide economical heating and cooling if they are operated only when the room they serve is occupied (bedroom units would run at night and living area units during the day). Installing several HVAC units allows one unit to fail without making the whole house uncomfortable.

Disadvantages of this option are noisy equipment, wasted floor space in each room, and the appearance of outdoor heat exchangers (see Figure 4.25).

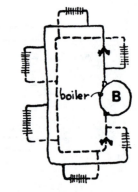
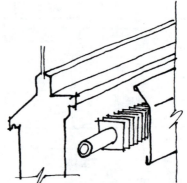

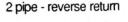

Convector   2 pipe - reverse return

FIGURE 4.24

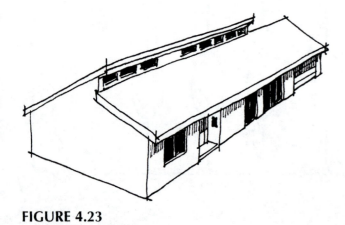

FIGURE 4.23

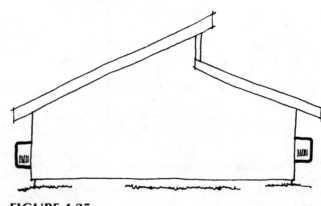

FIGURE 4.25

OPTION 3: SINGLE ZONE

A single-zone, constant volume installation is the usual choice for a house like this example (see Figure 4.26). Heating equipment can be a furnace or a heat pump. If a furnace is selected, the cooling equipment will probably be a split system, DX unit, with an air-cooled condensing unit located outdoors.

Supply ducts for the installation will run from the furnace or heat pump to a register in each room. Ducts are usually run overhead in hot climates and under the floor in cold climates (with outlets below windows). Ducts are insulated as necessary to prevent condensation, and good designers keep ducts out of unconditioned crawl spaces or attics.

Return air is drawn from rooms by undercutting doors but this reduces acoustical privacy. Outdoor air is provided by infiltration or by opening windows.

OPTION 4: RADIANT HEAT PLUS ZONED COOLING

This is an expensive, high-performance installation. Heating is radiant. Embedded tubing maintains the floor slab at 85°F providing quiet, efficient, draft-free heat. The radiant floor will keep a family comfortable through a very cold winter when good double- or triple-glass windows are specified to minimize the drafts single-glass windows create (see Figure 4.27).

Summer cooling is accomplished with two single-zone constant volume air-conditioning units (see Figure 4.28). One serves the bedrooms and the other serves the living areas. Two units permit different temperature settings and operating schedules for the rooms they

serve. Supply ducts are oversized, and two registers serve each space to minimize air stream noise. Return air is carried in insulated return ducts to ensure acoustical privacy. Outdoor air intakes with sensor-controlled dampers blend fresh air into the return air stream, and when weather conditions are ideal, 100% fresh air is used (see Figure 4.29). Electrostatic filters are installed on each air handler to minimize interior dust.

With separate heating and cooling equipment, ducted return, fresh air intakes, and electrostatic filters this installation is expensive. But it offers more flexibility, better control, greater comfort, and less noise than the three preceding options.

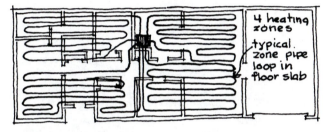

Radiant floor, 4 zones

FIGURE 4.27

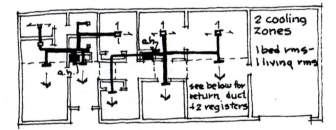

Cooling, 2 CV zones

FIGURE 4.28

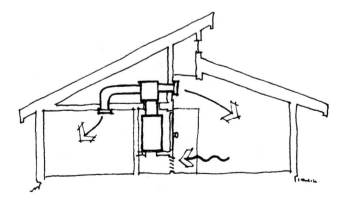

Option 3 schematic

FIGURE 4.26

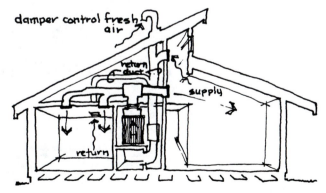

Option 4 schematic

FIGURE 4.29

4.7 OFFICE EXAMPLE, ZONING OPTIONS

Air-conditioning equipment options for the example office building (see Figure 4.30) include heat pumps, furnaces with DX cooling, or boilers and chillers. This case study emphasizes zoning choices instead of heating-cooling equipment selection. Four possible zoning options are considered.

OPTION 1: ZONED, MANY UNITS

This option provides many single-zone units with individual air handlers located above the suspended ceiling (see Figure 4.31). The building owner sets a mini-

mum rental area and specifies a heat pump to serve each tenant. Advantages of this option include minimum floor area for HVAC, individual temperature control for each tenant, and separate tenant billing for HVAC utilities. If a heat pump fails, only one tenant is disturbed. A disadvantage is difficult service access to air handlers located above the ceiling.

There are at least two other equipment types that will work with this option. A central boiler and chiller could serve ceiling-mounted air handlers in each rental space, or rooftop package units with furnaces could be substituted for the heat pumps.

Disadvantages of the boiler-chiller installation include excess capacity for limited night and weekend occupancy. A boiler or chiller failure could shut down the entire building. Disadvantages of rooftop package equipment include the loss of second-floor rental area because of ducts serving the first floor, and heating-cooling losses caused by circulating conditioned air through the poorly insulated rooftop units.

OPTION 2: ZONED, FOUR UNITS

This option assumes the building is occupied by one or two major tenants with open office plans. The building is divided into four zones (two on each floor) because of anticipated environmental heating and cooling loads. North and south sides of the building are separated to reflect different solar gains through windows (see Figure 4.32). First and second floors are separated because only the second floor experiences roof heat gain and loss. Each zone is served by a single, constant volume air handler.

An advantage of this option is easy service access to air handlers. Disadvantages include the need to operate large equipment to serve reduced night or weekend occupancy, and also a large building area will be affected if an air handler fails. Heat pumps, furnaces with DX cooling units, or boilers and chillers can be used as heat sources and sinks for the four air handlers.

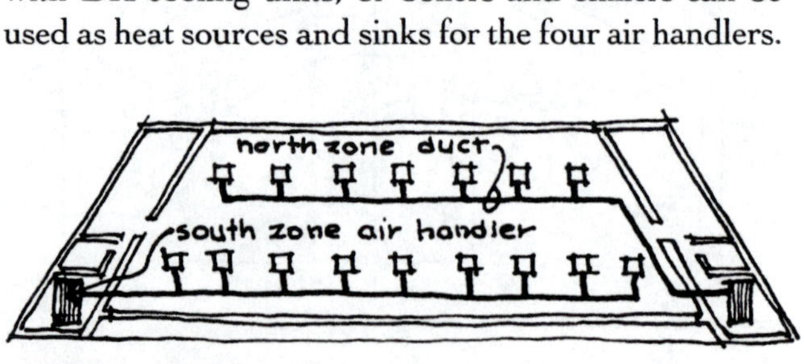

FIGURE 4.30

Option 1 Zoned Many AH

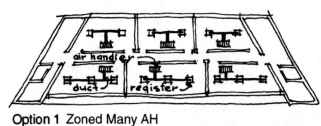

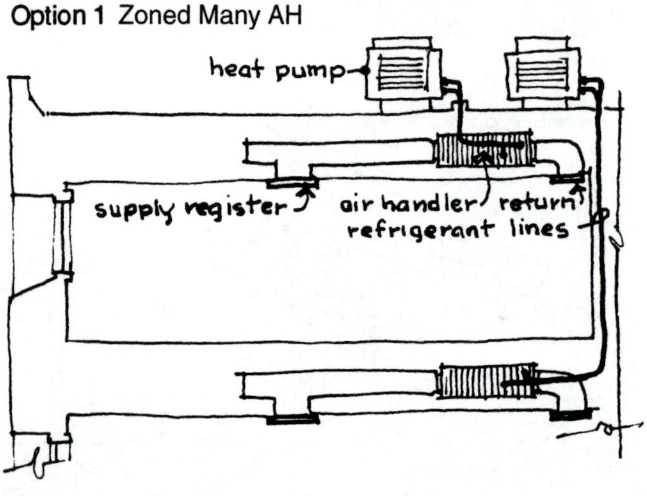

Option 1, schematic
FIGURE 4.31

Option 2 Zoned 4 AH
FIGURE 4.32

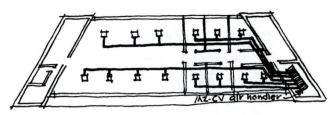

Option 3, MZ Individual Duct
FIGURE 4.33

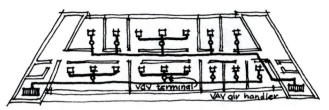

Option 4 Zoned VAV
FIGURE 4.34

OPTION 3: MULTIZONE

A single air handler can serve the entire building delivering warm or cool air to building spaces as dictated by individual thermostats (see Figure 4.33). The equipment delivers a constant volume of air to each outlet and varies air temperature to control space conditions. Many ducts are required to serve the building's four environmental zones and permit temperature choices for each tenant. *Individual duct bypass* multizone air handlers are specified to avoid mixing and to maximize operating efficiency. Duct work will require more space than the preceding options because a separate duct is required to serve each zone.

The advantage of this option is very good temperature control. Disadvantages are high first cost and loss of all heating and cooling should the air handler or the heating cooling equipment fail.

OPTION 4: ZONED, FOUR VAV UNITS

This option cuts the building into four environmental zones because concurrent heating and cooling may be required during spring and fall months (a single VAV air handler cannot provide simultaneous heat-

ing and cooling). Separate VAV air handlers are installed to serve the north and south sides of each floor. The air handlers vary air quantity to control space temperature. It is possible to heat with one air handler while another is cooling (see Figure 4.34).

Careful readers will note this option is identical to Option 2 except for VAV. In fact, VAV could be used with all the preceding options. The potential advantage of a VAV installation is reduced fan energy, particularly when the building is partially occupied on nights or weekends. Disadvantages are the loss of conditioning for a large area should an air handler fail and possible inadequate air motion in conditioned spaces when VAV fans reduce air quantity during partial load hours. VAV installations with fan-powered terminals are a popular zoning technique, but real operating cost savings occur only with a comprehensive and well-designed control system.

BEST ZONING OPTION?

Good arguments can be made for each zoning option. For a given building the "best" option is the one that best meets tenant comfort requirements, operating cost estimates, and construction budget limits.

REVIEW PROBLEMS

1. Select the type of heating equipment likely to have the highest operating cost.
   a. oil furnace
   b. electric heat pump
   c. electric resistance (strip) heat
   d. natural gas–fired boiler

2. Select the type of heating equipment likely to provide the most comfortable indoor environment for occupants.
   a. convectors
   b. radiant
   c. warm air (or central air)
   d. wood stove

3. How much space should be allowed for air handlers on each floor of a multistory building?
   a. none (install above ceiling)
   b. 2%
   c. 4%
   d. 6%
   e. 10%

4. Boilers are used instead of furnaces in large buildings because:
   a. water holds heat longer than air
   b. boilers are cheaper than furnaces
   c. hot water will freeze faster than cold water
   d. fuel-fired boilers don't require flues
   e. water can carry heat more economically than air

5. Which of the following is *not* required for quality air-conditioning in a large HVAC installation?
   a. reheat terminals
   b. heating and cooling equipment
   c. supply and return air ducting or plenum space
   d. exhaust air control
   e. outdoor air intake

6. The most efficient individual unit installation for dormitory heating and cooling in a temperate climate would be:
   a. fan coils
   b. packaged units
   c. duct furnaces
   d. loop-connected heat pumps

7. The most efficient type of multizone air-conditioning installation is:
   a. MZ reheat
   b. MZ double duct
   c. MZ individual duct mixing
   d. MZ individual duct bypass

8. The least efficient type of multizone air-conditioning installation is:
   a. MZ reheat
   b. MZ double duct
   c. MZ individual duct mixing
   d. MZ individual duct bypass

9. Reheat can be an effective way to control humidity. Try to think of a situation where reheat can be an efficient air-conditioning technique.

10. The best equipment type for air-conditioning small rooms where acoustical privacy is critical would be:
    a. individual units
    b. single zone
    c. zoned
    d. multizone

11. Where acoustical privacy is an important consideration in a building with large air handlers a ducted __ should be specified.
    a. return
    b. exhaust
    c. fresh air intake
    d. boiler

12. An advantage of VAV (variable air volume) air handlers compared to constant volume is:
    a. improved temperature control
    b. improved humidity control
    c. improved air circulation
    d. reduced fan energy

Select answers for the next three questions from the following list (MZ = multizone; CV = constant volume; VAV = variable volume). You may use answers more than once.
    a. single zone, CV
    b. zoned VAV units
    c. MZ double duct, CV
    d. MZ reheat, CV
    e. MZ individual duct, CV, mixing

13. Lowest operating cost for a large office building?

14. Lowest first cost and good performance for a church seating 200?

15. Low first cost and good temperature control for many different spaces, but high operating cost?

ANSWERS

1. c
2. b (correct for good radiant floor installations but incorrect for an individual radiant heater which is about as comfortable as a wood stove)
3. c
4. e
5. a
6. d
7. d
8. a
9. "Economizer cycle" is a term for using outdoor air instead of refrigeration equipment to cool heat rich buildings. A problem with economizer operation is that sometimes outdoor air is too moist to do a good air-conditioning job. In this situation, reheat may be more economical than operating a chiller.

   A second efficient application of reheat is humidity control when the heat is "free." Waste heat rejected by the condenser of refrigeration equipment is a possible source.
10. a
11. a (a ducted return will minimize sound transmission typical in an open return plenum)
12. d
13. b
14. a
15. d

CHAPTER 5

Air Distribution

*When the autumn wind
scatters peonies, a few
petals fall in pairs.*

Buson

A somewhat different format is used in this chapter. Several tables are included in the text, and example problems are presented with each table. Work the examples as you read.

Following the tables is a presentation that develops a complete air distribution system for the house example used previously in Chapters 2 and 4. Refer back to the tables as you review illustrations and comments concerning air quantities, register selection, and duct sizing.

A discussion of fans and controls follows the illustrations on air distribution, and the chapter ends with review problems. When you complete this chapter you should be able to size, select, and specify all the components of a low-velocity air distribution system. This ability will permit you to make proper space allowances for air-conditioning most buildings.

Large buildings frequently use high-velocity air distribution systems to save space, but thoughtful designers allow adequate room for quieter low-velocity systems that use less fan energy. Carefully follow the air distribution example and when you understand this material use it as a guide to size and select registers and ducts for a building of your choice.

5.0 REGISTERS

Registers are outlets that distribute and control conditioned air. They include two components: a *diffuser* that spreads an air stream, and a *damper* to adjust air quantity (see Figure 5.1). Good registers have adjustable diffuser vanes and opposed blade dampers. Cheap registers have stamped diffuser vanes and multishutter dampers. Good registers are more expensive, but the small added cost buys quiet and complete distribution of conditioned air.

Registers are selected to distribute conditioned air without causing uncomfortable drafts. *Throw* is defined as the horizontal distance an air stream travels from a register before it slows to a velocity that is comfortable for people (usually 50 to 100 FPM). If a small register and a large register are delivering equal air quantities, the small register will provide a greater throw and make more noise (see Figure 5.2).

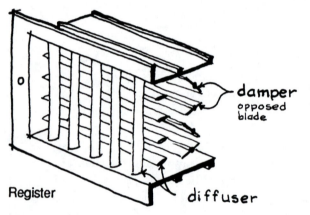

Register

FIGURE 5.1

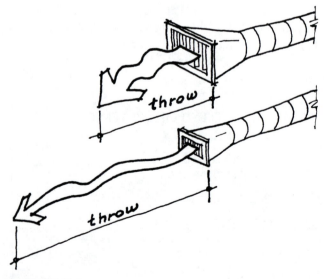

FIGURE 5.2

Register noise increases as throw increases. For quiet applications such as recording studios, designers increase the number of registers to minimize throw and noise.

WALL REGISTERS

Air distribution patterns for wall registers are straight, medium, and maximum (see Figure 5.3). Pick a pattern to distribute air throughout the conditioned space and select a throw of 75% of the distance to the far wall.

Selection Examples

1. Select a straight pattern wall register to throw 400 CFM a distance of 15 feet.
2. Select a maximum pattern wall register to throw 250 CFM a distance of 7 feet.
3. Select a medium pattern wall register to throw 700 CFM a distance of 15 feet.
4. Select a medium pattern wall register to throw 700 CFM a distance of 19 feet.

5–7. These three examples appear below Table 5.1 on page 77. Start by deciding the pattern. Figure the throw at 75% of the distance to the far wall. Select a register for each example.

Answers

1. Select 10×24.
2. Select 6×16 or 6×20.
3. Select 12×36.
4. Select 8×30 or 10×24 (the table indicates a throw of 20 feet—close enough).
5. Pattern = straight, throw = 12 feet, select 6×14.
6. Pattern = maximum, throw = 9 feet, select 8×20.
7. Pattern = medium, throw = 15 feet, select 8×24.

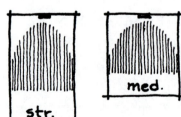

Wall Register Pattern

FIGURE 5.3

5.1 WALL REGISTER SELECTION

THROW *NOT* IN TABLE?

Throw information is omitted from Table 5.1 when air quantities fall above or below the working range of a given register. If no throw is given try using two registers at half CFM for each, but remember to revise the register pattern.

TABLE 5.1

Wall Register Size in Inches (size is opening dimension, actual register face is 2 to 3 inches larger)

CFM	4×8	4×10	4×12	6×10	6×12	6×14	6×16	6×20	6×24
50	3–6	3–5							
100	6–11	6–10	4–8	4–7					
125	7–13	6–12	5–10	5–9	4–8	4–7			
150			7–12	6–12	5–10	5–9			
175				7–13	6–11	6–10	5–9		
200				8–15	7–13	6–12	6–11	6–10	
225					8–15	8–14	7–12	6–11	
250					9–17	8–15	7–14	7–13	6–12
300						10–19	9–17	8–16	8–15
350							11–20	10–18	9–17
400								11–21	10–19
CFM	8×20	8×24	8×30	8×36	10×24	10×30	10×36	12×30	12×36
400	9–18	8–16			7–15				
500	12–22	10–20	9–18		9–18	8–16			
600	14–26	13–24	12–22	11–20	12–22	10–18	9–17		
700	16–31	15–29	14–26	13–23	14–26	12–23	11–21	11–21	10–20
800	19–35	17–32	16–29	14–26	16–29	14–26	13–24	13–24	12–22
900		19–36	17–32	16–30	17–32	15–29	14–27	14–27	13–25
1,000			19–36	18–34	19–36	18–32	17–30	17–30	15–26
1,200				21–40		21–38	19–35	19–35	17–33

Table field numbers are register throws (in feet). The *low number* is the throw for a *maximum* pattern register. The *high number* is the throw for a *straight* pattern register. *Interpolate for medium* pattern registers. Design throw dimension is 3/4 of the distance to the far wall.

Examples:

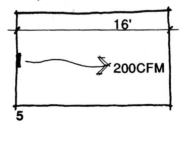

16'

200CFM

5

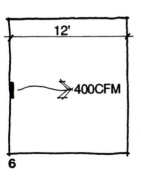

12'

400CFM

6

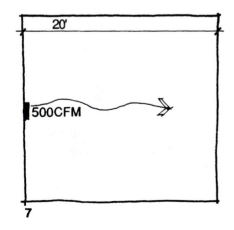

20'

500CFM

7

5.2 CEILING REGISTERS

Tables 5.2, 5.3 and 5.4 provide throw distances for one way, two way, and four way square ceiling registers. Pick a pattern to distribute air throughout the conditioned space and select a throw equal to the distance **to the far wall.**

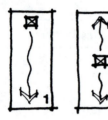 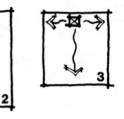

Examples

Cover the answers next to the examples and select the appropriate pattern, throw, and size for each.

CFM: 700
Pattern: One Way
Throw: 30 feet
Select **15×15**

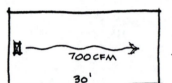

CFM: 700
Pattern: Two Way
Throw: 15 feet
Select **21×21**

CFM: 700
Pattern: Four Way
Throw: 15 feet
Select **15×15**

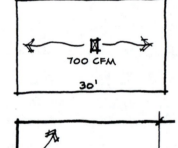

Danger! Use manufacturers' catalogs. CFMs and throws given here are generic. Register characteristics vary a lot from one manufacturer to another, so verify all CFM and throw data with your supplier before placing an order. Add a Hart & Cooley or Titus catalog to your library and use it instead of these pages. Both manufacture quality register lines and they include the three-way patterns missing here.

TABLE 5.2

One-Way Square Register Size (throw to far wall)

Size	6	9	12	15	18	21	24
CFM							
100	11	8					
125		9					
150		10					
175		12	9				
200		15	11				
250			13				
300			16				
400		22	18	14			
500			22	18			
600			26	21			
700			30	25	21		
800				29	25	21	
900				32	28	24	

TABLE 5.3

Two-Way Square Register Size (throw to far wall)

Size	6	9	12	15	18	21	24
CFM							
100	7	5					
125		6					
150		8	5				
175		9	6				
200		10	7				
250			9	7			
300		11	9	7			
400			12	10			
500			15	13			
600			19	15	13		
700			22	18	15	13	
800				20	18	15	
900				23	20	17	

TABLE 5.4

Four-Way Square Register Size (throw to far wall)

Size	6	9	12	15	18	21	24
CFM							
75	4						
100	6	4					
125	7	5					
150		5					
175		6	4				
200		7	5				
225		8	6				
250			7	5			
300			8	7			
400			11	9	7		
500				11	9	7	
600				13	11	9	
700				15	13	11	9
800					14	13	11
900					16	14	13
1,000					18	16	14
1,200						19	17

Field numbers are throw in feet.

5.3 FLOOR AND RETURN REGISTERS

FLOOR REGISTERS

Select floor registers so that their throw covers the vertical distance from the register to the ceiling (see Figure 5.4). Floor registers are often installed below windows to minimize cold winter drafts and to prevent condensation on glass.

RETURN AIR GRILLES

Sizes in Table 5.6 are for fairly quiet installations. Remember to provide ducts or a plenum for return air flow to the air handler. *Filter grilles* (return grilles with filters) can simplify filter maintenance when access to the air handler is difficult.

FLOOR AND RETURN REGISTER SELECTION

Select floor registers and return grilles for the following example problems using Tables 5.5 and 5.6.

1. Select a floor register for the room shown in Figure 5.5.
   Answer: Select a 3″ register 6′ long. It will deliver 600 CFM with a throw of 14 feet. You may add inactive register lengths if desired for aesthetic reasons. Best register location is below windows to minimize winter convective drafts.

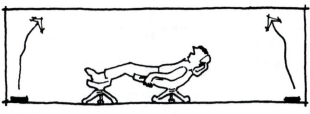

FIGURE 5.4

2. Select a register for the room in the preceding example located in a 3′ high base cabinet.
   Answer: Select a 2″ register 10′ long. By interpolation each foot will deliver 59 CFM with a throw of 11′ (590 CFM = nearly 600).
3. Select a return grille for the preceding example room.
   Answer: Select 12×18. Size to return all supply air. Oversize return grilles to minimize air stream noise.
4. Select a return air filter grille for a 2-ton air conditioner.
   Answer: Refer ahead to page 84. Two tons at 400 CFM per ton = 800 CFM. Select 16×20.

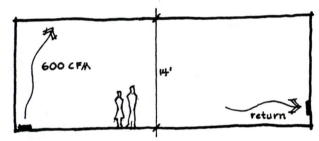

FIGURE 5.5

TABLE 5.5

Floor Registers: CFM for 1 Foot Length

Throw = ceiling height (above register)

Throw	6′	8′	10′	12′	14′	16′	20′
Size							
1 1/2″	27	36	42	54			
2″	34	44	54	64	78		
2 1/2″	42	50	60	73	86	100	
3″		60	71	86	100	112	
3 1/2″		67	76	89	105	118	
4″			88	98	114	132	160
5″			104	121	138	156	185
6″			129	150	170	190	230

TABLE 5.6

Return Grilles

Size	CFM	Size	CFM
6×12	250	24×30	2,000
12×12	500	30×30	2,500
12×18	700	30×36	3,000
12×24	900	24×48	3,200
20×24	1,400	36×48	4,800
24×24	1,700	48×48	6,000

Return Filter Grilles

Size	CFM	Size	CFM
16×20	800	20×25	1,200
20×20	1,000	20×30	1,400
16×25	1,000		

5.4 DUCT SIZING

STATIC REGAIN

A duct system is "balanced" when the design air quantity flows from each outlet. Duct system designers understand the tendency for outlets near a fan to deliver more air than outlets distant from a fan because of duct friction. The *static regain method* is the most accurate way of sizing a well-balanced duct system. Static regain calculations adjust duct size to obtain equal static pressure and correct air quantity at each outlet.

The total pressure in a duct is the sum of static and velocity pressures (see Figure 5.6). Static pressure is the outward push of air against duct surfaces as a result of the fan's compressive action. Velocity pressure is the directional push of an air stream due to its speed. It is possible to trade static pressure and velocity pressure by changing duct size. A decrease in duct size forces air speed and velocity pressure to increase as static pressure decreases. Enlarging a duct will cause air speed and velocity pressure to decrease as static pressure increases (see Figure 5.7).

EQUAL FRICTION

Static regain calculations are complex because friction losses must be established for all elbows, transitions, and other components of the duct system.

The duct size chart in Table 5.7 on page 81 is based on a simpler (and less accurate) method of duct sizing called *equal friction*.

The equal friction method of duct sizing can be used for low-velocity duct systems with a duct length of 100 feet or less. Ducts are selected by assuming a total friction loss of 1/10" of water. Duct system performance approximates static regain, but extractors and dampers are required to ensure balanced air distribution.

Examples

Use Table 5.7 to select airway dimensions for ducts. *Airway* means inside dimensions.

1. Select a round duct to carry 1,000 CFM.
2. Select a rectangular duct to carry 1,000 CFM.
3. A 16×12 duct carrying 1,000 CFM—duct must divide into two ducts which will carry 600 CFM and 400 CFM respectively. Select sizes for these two ducts.

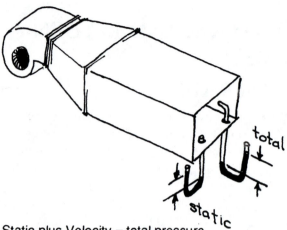

Static plus Velocity = total pressure
FIGURE 5.6

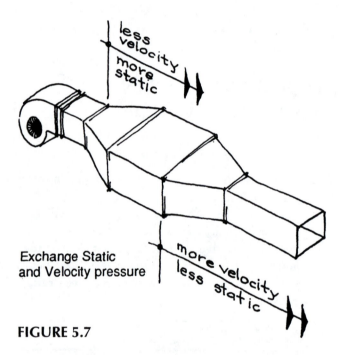

Exchange Static and Velocity pressure

FIGURE 5.7

4. Select a rectangular duct to carry 6,000 CFM.
5. Select an insulated rectangular duct to carry 6,000 CFM through a 19" high space.
6. The 40×16 duct from the preceding example must be run vertically to serve a floor above. Size the vertical duct section to fit in a 30" square chase.

Answers

1. 14" diameter
2. 12×14 (Always select rectangular duct sizes that are nearly square if you have enough space to accommodate them. Square ducts can be fabricated with less material.)

TABLE 5.7

Duct Size (CFM = cubic feet of air per minute)

CFM	Round	Rectangular Duct Size								
50	5	4×4	6×3							
100	6	4×7	6×5	8×4						
150	7	4×10	6×7	8×5	10×4					
200	8	4×12	6×8	8×6	10×5	12×4				
250	8		6×10	8×7	10×6	12×5				
300	9		6×11	8×8	10×7	12×6	14×5			
350	10		6×13	8×9	10×7	12×6	14×6			
400	10		6×14	8×10	10×8	12×7	14×6			
500	12		6×16	8×12	10×10	12×8	14×7	16×6		
600	12		6×20	8×14	10×12	12×10	14×8	16×7		
700	12			8×16	10×12	12×10	14×9	16×8		
800	14			8×18	10×14	12×12	14×10	16×9	18×8	
900	14			8×20	10×16	12×12	14×10	16×9	18×9	
1,000	14			8×22	10×16	12×14	14×12	16×10	18×9	
1,200	16			8×24	10×18	12×16	14×14	16×12	18×10	
1,400	16				10×20	12×18	14×16	16×14	18×12	20×10
1,600	18				10×24	12×20	14×18	16×14	18×14	20×12
1,800	18				10×26	12×20	14×18	16×16	18×14	20×12
2,000	18				10×30	12×24	14×20	16×18	18×16	20×14
2,500	20	20×16	24×14	28×12	32×12	36×10				
3,000	22	20×18	24×16	28×14	32×12	36×12				
4,000	24	20×24	24×20	28×16	32×16	36×14				
6,000	28	20×32	24×26	28×22	32×20	36×18	40×16			
8,000	32	20×40	24×34	28×28	32×26	36×22	40×20	48×18		
10,000	34	20×48	24×40	28×32	32×28	36×26	40×24	48×20		
20,000	44		24×70	28×60	32×50	36×46	40×40	48×34	60×20	
40,000	60						40×80	48×66	60×52	
80,000	90								60×100+	

Notes:
- Dimensions are given in inches for the airway *inside* the duct. Most ducts are insulated to prevent condensation and minimize heat gain or loss. To determine outside duct dimensions add two times the thickness of the duct insulation specified (standard duct insulation thicknesses are 1/2", 1", and 2"). Duct sizes assume a friction loss of 1/10" of water per 100' of length.
- Duct sizes given are only for low-velocity duct systems (less than 2,000 FPM air velocity). The maximum length of low-velocity supply duct runs is about 200'.
- Size return air ducts 2" larger than supply ducts.

3. 7×12 and 10×12 (Where space permits hold one dimension of the original duct. This permits easier fabrication of the transition.)
4. 24×26
5. 40×16 (Always give plan dimension of the duct first; 40×16 duct is 42×18 outside dimension with 1" thick duct insulation.)
6. 24×26 (nearest square fit)

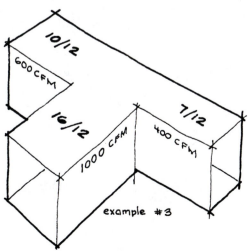

example #3

81

5.5 DUCT MATERIALS AND FABRICATION

Most rectangular ducts are fabricated from galvanized steel or foil-faced fiberglass. Fiberglass ducts are self-insulating. Insulation is applied to steel ducts to minimize heat loss, heat gain, and condensation. Insulating the inside surfaces of steel ducts cuts sound transmission and simplifies duct supports with a slight increase in duct friction.

STEEL

"Pittsburgh," (see Figure 5.8) snap lock, spiral lock, and flanged connections are used to connect steel duct sections. Pittsburgh joints permit ducts to be shipped flat and ease site assembly.

Metal thickness (gauge), support spacing, and connection types for various applications should meet SMACNA specifications (Sheet Metal & Air Conditioning Contractors National Association).

FIBERGLASS

Foil-faced fiberglass ducts are easier to fabricate than steel ducts (see Figure 5.9). Sheets of 1″ or 1 1/2″ duct board are cut with a razor knife and folded to size. End joints have an interlocking edge that is sealed with heat-sensitive tape.

Round rigid fiberglass ducts are also available in diameters from 4″ through 30″, and fiberglass duct liner in thicknesses from 1/2″ to 2″ is used in steel ducts.

ROUND AND ELLIPTICAL

Round steel ducts are fabricated in light gauge sections with longitudinal joints or in heavier gauges using spiral lock joints. A variety of standard fittings are available for changing duct size and direction.

A circle is the most efficient duct shape in terms of material required and friction loss, but round ducts are sometimes rolled to elliptical shapes to reduce duct height where vertical clearance is limited. When round duct work is a visible design feature, insulated duct with a perforated internal steel liner to minimize air stream noise is often specified (see Figure 5.10).

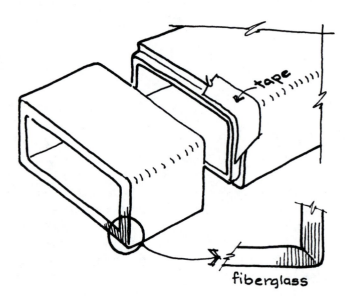

FIGURE 5.9

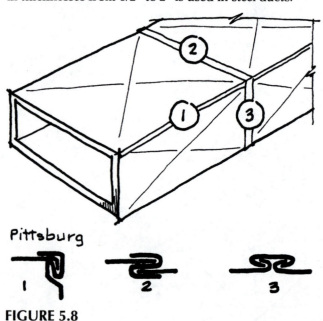

FIGURE 5.8

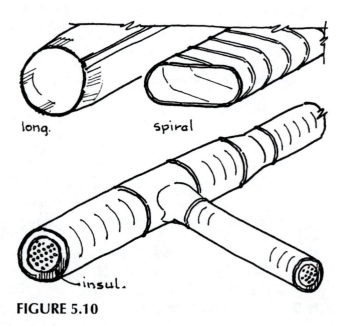

FIGURE 5.10

FULL RADIUS

The drawings in Figures 5.11 and 5.12 illustrate full-radius and right angle duct configurations. Full-radius bends minimize duct friction and turbulent air flow. They require a lot of material and space but they are the preferred bend type in quiet quality installations.

Right angle bends are cheaper than full-radius bends, but they are noisy and require more fan energy to overcome increased duct friction. Turning vanes are installed in right angle bends to limit turbulent air flow. Extractors are required at right angle branches to balance air flow.

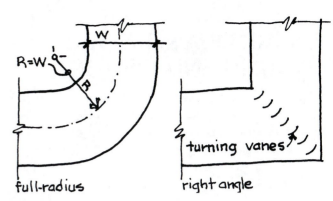

FIGURE 5.11

HVAC PLAN

The view in Figure 5.13 is a partial plan of a typical supply and return duct installation. Dotted lines at wall registers locate a ceiling break. What do dotted lines on the return duct indicate?

+ Duct sizes are noted plan dimension first.
+ Supply and return registers and grilles are emphasized with the heaviest line weight.
+ CFM, size, and pattern are noted for each register.
+ Extra clearance is required where the return duct crosses the supply duct.

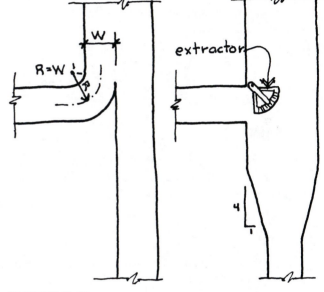

FIGURE 5.12

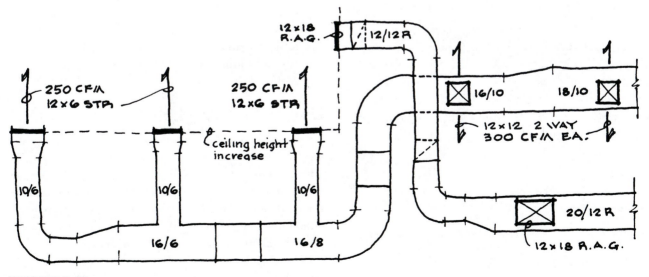

FIGURE 5.13

5.6 AIR QUANTITY FOR HEATING AND COOLING

Heating-cooling systems use air to carry heat from one location to another. The quantity of air circulated in a duct system is determined by the quantity of heating or cooling required and by the temperature difference between conditioned air and room air. The following equation is used to determine air quantity:

$$RSH/(1.08)(TD) = CFM$$

RSH (room sensible* heat) is the amount of sensible heat that must be added or removed to maintain room temperature (in BTUH).
1.08 is the sensible heat content of air (p. 15).
TD is the temperature difference between conditioned air and room air.
CFM is the quantity of air in cubic feet per minute.

EXAMPLE 1

A room has a peak winter sensible heat loss of 25,000 BTUH. How much 130°F air must be supplied to maintain room temperature at 70°F?

$$RSH/(1.08)(TD) = CFM$$
$$25,000/1.08(130-70) = \qquad \textbf{386 CFM}$$

The same room has a summer peak sensible heat gain of 15,000 BTUH. How much 55°F air is required to maintain 75°F in the room?

$$RSH/(1.08)(TD) = CFM$$
$$15,000/1.08(75-55) = \qquad \textbf{694 CFM}$$

Note that summer cooling requires more conditioned air than winter heating even though heat loss exceeds heat gain. This is usually true due to the smaller TD typical in cooling operations. However, heat pumps deliver warm air in the 80° to 110°F range, and heating requirements may determine air quantity when heat pumps are used.

---

*Sensible heat is measured with a dry-bulb thermometer; air quantities for heating or cooling are determined by sensible heat loads.

Latent heat, the phase change heat held in water vapor, is removed when water condenses on a cooling coil. When latent heat is a large part of the total cooling load, larger cooling coils are specified to reduce air velocity and increase the condensing surface area.

EXAMPLE 2

Calculate the quantity of heating and cooling air required for the following room:

Winter RSH = 35,000 BTUH; supply air is 100°F; room temperature is 65°F.
Summer RSH = 20,000 BTUH; supply air is 55°F; room temperature is 75°F.

Does heating or cooling set air quantity requirements for the room above?

Answer:
Heating air required
$$35,000/1.08(100-65) = \qquad \textbf{926 CFM}$$
Cooling air required
$$20,000/1.08(75-55) = \qquad \textbf{926 CFM}$$

Heating and cooling CFM are equal in this example.

400 CFM PER TON

One ton of air-conditioning capacity is defined as a heat removal rate of 12,000 BTUH, and each ton of air-conditioning load usually includes a sensible* component of 8,000 to 9,000 BTUH. Air handlers typically circulate about 400 CFM for each ton of capacity.

FOUR STEPS FOR AIR DISTRIBUTION

If you have not calculated sensible heat loads for each room in a building and you need a good preliminary estimate for conditioned air quantity, proceed as follows:

1. Multiply total tons by 400 to estimate total CFM.
2. Distribute CFM in proportion to floor area.
3. Adjust CFM to reflect anticipated variations in RSH due to specific building conditions (p. 15).
4. Round off air supply for each room to nearest 25 CFM.

DUCT EXAMPLES

Section 5.7 provides examples of air distribution, register selection, and duct sizing for the example house used in previous heat loss and gain calculations. Study the drawings and text until you understand the air distribution process and then prepare a schematic duct plan for the west half of the house. This air distribution method can also be used for commercial buildings like the example office, and similar low-velocity air-conditioning installations.

5.7 HOUSE EXAMPLE, AIR DISTRIBUTION

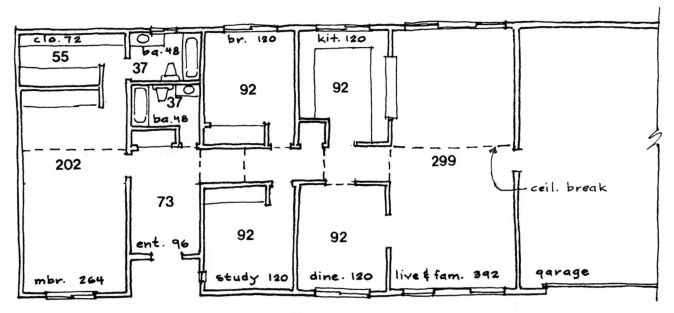

The plan above illustrates steps 1 and 2 of the air distribution method described in Section 5.6. The house example above has a floor area of 1,528 sq. ft. and a peak heat gain of 33,537 BTUH. A 36,000 BTUH (3-ton) cooling unit will be used because it is the standard equipment size closest to the peak cooling load. The 3-ton air conditioner will circulate about 1,200 CFM (400 CFM per ton).

Room areas in square feet are shown next to room names. CFM distribution, based on room area, is shown in the center of each room (1,200 CFM ÷ 1,568 sq. ft. = 0.76 CFM per sq. ft.).

On the plan below, room CFM have been adjusted in accordance with steps 3 and 4 to reflect variations in anticipated RSH (room sensible heat).

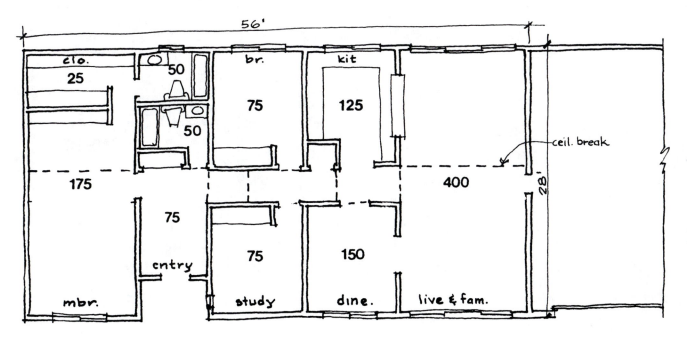

Adjustments were made as follows:

Bedrooms and study: Decrease CFM because of smaller glass area and cooler nights.
Dining: Increase CFM because of more potential occupants.
Kitchen: Increase CFM because of cooking.
Living and family: Increase CFM because of occupants and glass area.

Readers who desire more precise air quantity adjustments will calculate sensible heat gain for each room (RSH) and use the equation: CFM = RSH/1.08 TD.

Both ceiling and wall registers will be used to deliver conditioned air in the example house. Ceiling registers will serve the 8′ high spaces. They are sized to throw air to the surrounding walls. Wall registers will be used to serve the spaces with high walls and cathedral ceilings. They are sized to throw air 75% of the distance to the far wall. Register patterns are selected to distribute conditioned air throughout each room. The schematic section in Figure 5.14 shows register and duct location.

Registers shown on the plan in Figure 5.15 were selected using Tables 5.1 through 5.6. Selection was based on the CFM, pattern, and the throw necessary to cool each room. Designers may select alternate register shapes as long as the required throw distance is maintained. For example a 4×18 can replace a 6×12. Wall registers are shown as a rectangle and ceiling registers as a square. The numbers near each register are CFM, throw, and pattern, and the underlined numbers are register size. Review the air quantities on page 85 and verify the register selections in Figure 5.15 by referring back to Tables 5.1 through 5.6.

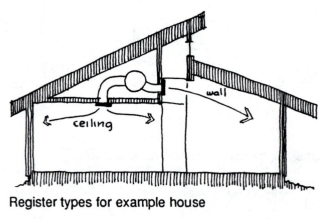

Register types for example house

FIGURE 5.14

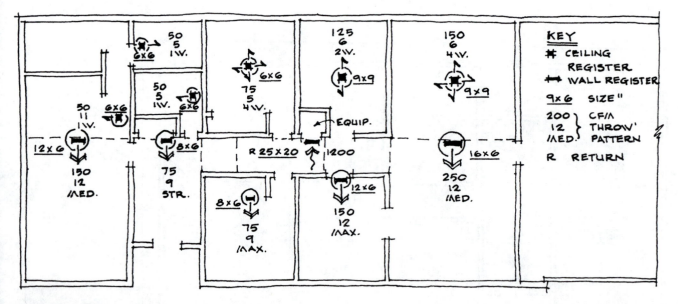

Register Size, CFM, Throw, and Pattern

FIGURE 5.15

The plan below shows a schematic round duct layout for the house example. Duct sizes were selected using Table 5.7. Check the results by working from the last outlet back to the air handler increasing duct size as CFM increases.

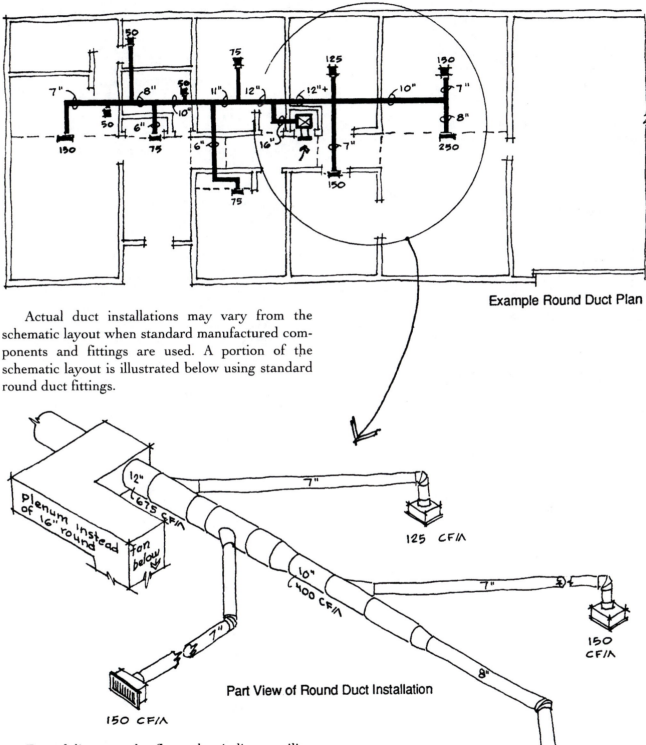

Example Round Duct Plan

Actual duct installations may vary from the schematic layout when standard manufactured components and fittings are used. A portion of the schematic layout is illustrated below using standard round duct fittings.

Part View of Round Duct Installation

Dotted lines on the floor plan indicate ceiling height changes. Two low ceiling areas bridge the hall to provide a duct route serving the study and dining room. Ceiling height changes are design opportunities that can complement clerestory lighting and room proportions.

Round duct provides the most efficient duct shape in terms of duct material and friction loss (see Figure 5.16). But because round duct requires more vertical space (and building height), rectangular duct is often substituted. *Aspect ratio* is the ratio of width to height for rectangular duct. Limiting rectangular duct aspect ratios to 3:1 or less will limit material waste and friction losses.

The schematics on page 89 illustrate conversion of round duct to rectangular duct for the house example. Rectangular ducts will be fabricated with 1″ thick insulation, and a maximum duct height of 10″ is assumed. Duct sizes shown are inside *airway* dimensions. Actual outside dimensions of the ducts will be 2″ greater than the airway dimensions because of insulation thickness.

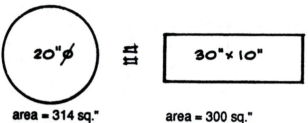

area = 314 sq."
surface = 63"

area = 300 sq."
surface = 80"

FIGURE 5.16

The following checklist explains considerations and details of the rectangular duct conversion:

1. Duct plan or width dimension is noted before duct height. The rule is, "note the dimension that is visible in a drawing first." Therefore, width is noted first in a plan view but height is noted first in a section or elevation view.
2. Ducts larger than 12″ are fabricated in even inches, i.e., 22×18 instead of 22×17.
3. Reductions in duct size are made with a gentle slope to avoid air turbulence—1:4 slope is a recommended maximum.
4. Ducts extend one duct width past ceiling registers to reduce air turbulence and noise.
5. Ducts are insulated to reduce heat loss or gain and to prevent condensation. When insulation is installed inside ducts it will also reduce air stream noise.
6. Branch duct sizes are selected so that the width of the duct equals the width of the register they serve.
7. Duct work in commercial buildings would include extractors at the two right angle branches nearest the air handler, and turning vanes in the end tee (so would a good residential installation).

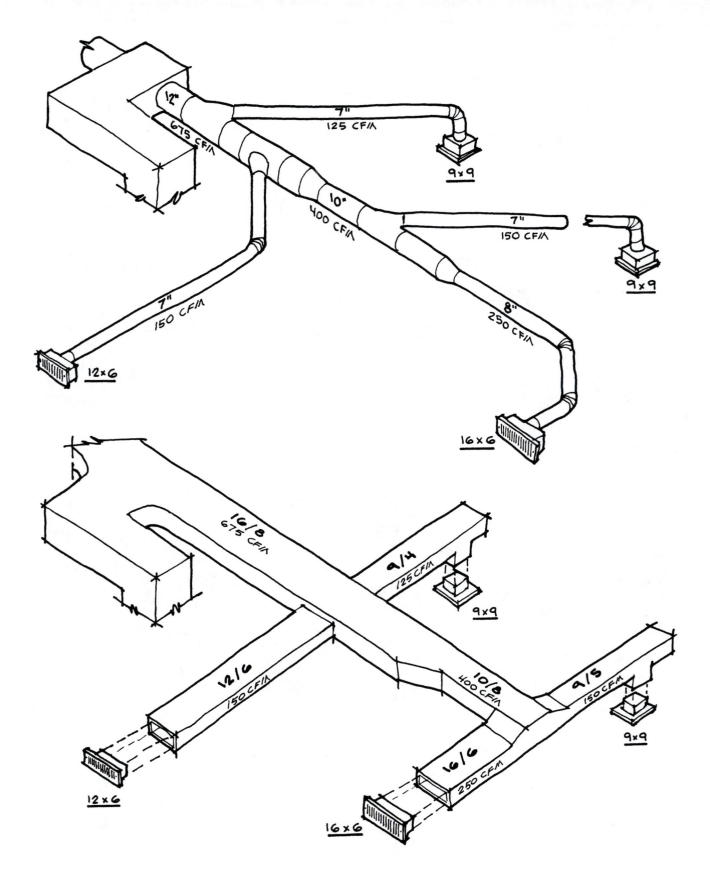

Example; convert round duct to rectangular duct

5.8 FANS

PRESSURE, VELOCITY, AND QUANTITY

In duct systems, pressure and fan load are measured in inches of water (see Figure 5.17). Air speed is measured in FPM (feet per minute) and air quantity is measured in CFM (cubic feet per minute).

Fans are similar to water pumps in that the amount of fluid they move varies with the load they overcome. Fan load is caused by friction as air moves through ducts, elbows, dampers, coils, registers, grilles, and filters. Duct system friction load increases with increasing air velocity.

FAN TYPES

Most air-conditioning installations use fans to distribute conditioned air. Centrifugal (rotating wheel) or axial (propeller) fan types are used (see Figure 5.18).

Centrifugal

Centrifugal fans offer quiet efficient air distribution for ducted installations. Residential and small commercial installations use forward curved blades on the fan wheel. Larger buildings use backward curved fan blades because of their increased efficiency. The most efficient centrifugal fan blade design is the airfoil shape. It delivers the greatest air quantity per unit of energy input.

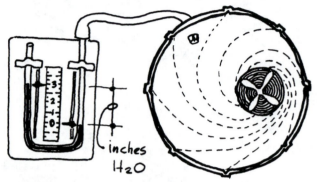

Pressure in fan and duct systems
FIGURE 5.17

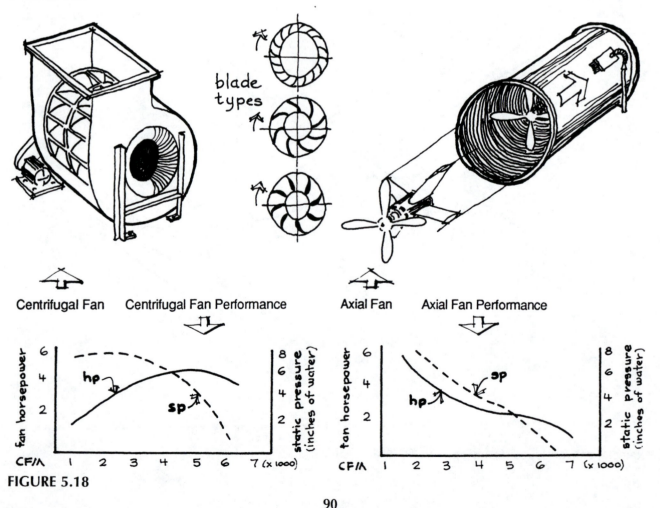

Centrifugal Fan   Centrifugal Fan Performance

Axial Fan   Axial Fan Performance

FIGURE 5.18

Axial

Axial fans are efficient moving large quantities of air in open applications such as building exhaust. Recent design improvements also permit axial fans to be used in some ducted installations.

ACTUAL CFM

The actual quantity of air delivered by a fan/duct system is determined by superimposing the fan performance curve on the pressure profile for the duct system (see Figure 5.19). The duct system profile will show increasing pressure (due to friction) as system CFM increases. Actual CFM will be found at the intersection of the duct pressure profile and the fan performance curve. As a first guess estimate of actual CFM in a low-velocity system look at the 0.3″ to 0.5″ pressure range of the fan curve.

VARIABLE VOLUME

Variable volume fans save energy by varying CFM (and fan power input) in response to variations in a building's heating or cooling load. Air quantity and fan energy can be decreased using inlet dampers, varying blade pitch, or controlling fan speed. Electronic motor speed control offers the greatest potential energy savings. Inlet dampers don't conserve energy (see Figure 5.20).

HIGH VELOCITY OR LOW VELOCITY

Large buildings use high-velocity air distribution to reduce duct size (and building space required for ducts). High-velocity installations include stronger ducts, sound attenuators, velocity-reducing terminals, and more powerful fans (see Table 5.8).

High-velocity air distribution wastes energy and should be avoided whenever possible. Low-velocity air handlers can deliver conditioned air economically as far as 200 feet from the fan room. Where 200 feet is inadequate, consider a second low-velocity air handler instead of a high-velocity system.

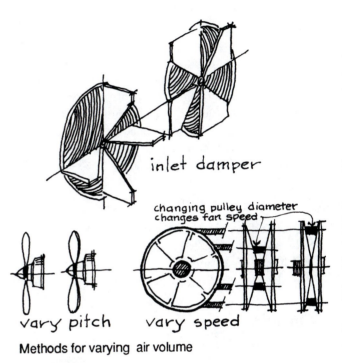

Methods for varying air volume

FIGURE 5.20

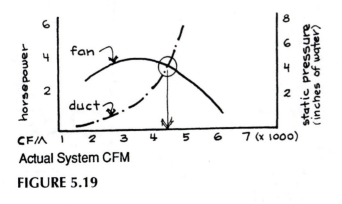

Actual System CFM

FIGURE 5.19

TABLE 5.8

Pressure and Velocity

Name	Air Speed	Inches H₂O
Low pressure (low velocity)	Under 2,000 FPM	Under 2″
Medium pressure (medium velocity)	Over 2,000 FPM	2″ to 6″
High pressure (high velocity)	Over 2,000 FPM	6″ to 10″

5.9 HVAC CONTROLS

First-time builders spend thousands of dollars for air-conditioning equipment and then try to reduce total building costs by purchasing the cheapest controls available. An air-conditioning installation is only as good as its controls, and control "cost cutting" always cuts occupant comfort and possibly occupant productivity.

Several fine companies operate divisions that specialize in building HVAC controls and devices. Designers, constructors, and owners are well advised when they employ competent control consultants and rely on their advice and recommendations concerning control type and function. "Smart" buildings rely on state-of-the-art control subsystems to maintain comfortable conditions and conserve energy (see Figure 5.21).

TYPES OF CONTROL

On-off and proportional are two types of control typically used with building air-conditioning equipment (see Figures 5.22 and 5.23). The following paragraphs describe each type briefly beginning with the simplest.

On-Off

On-off control is typical of most residential heating-cooling systems. The heating or cooling equipment starts and operates at full capacity until the requirement for heating or cooling is satisfied. Temperature in the controlled spaces is continually changing around a set point and the magnitude of this change is called "swing" or "control differential."

On-off type control (and open-closed control for valves) is also used in large commercial buildings for specific applications. An air handler that is designed for immediate changeover from heating to cooling will use open-closed control for hot and chill water supply valves.

Proportional

Proportional control offers more precise control of temperature and humidity than on-off control. Proportional controls continually adjust the position of valves and dampers to maintain design temperature and humidity with minimum swing.

CONTROLS

HVAC control installations include three elements: sensors, signal switches and media, and controlled devices. Sometimes all three components are incorporated in a single device like a pressure relief valve that senses and operates without outside help. More often the control components are separate interconnected parts.

Sensors

Sensors respond to changes in temperature, pressure or velocity, and humidity by moving or by changing the resistance of an electric circuit. Mechanical temperature sensors move because of the expansion or contraction of a metal element or gas. Pressure or ve-

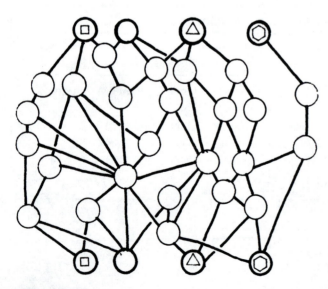

FIGURE 5.21

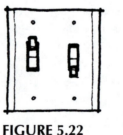

FIGURE 5.22

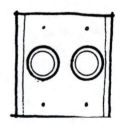

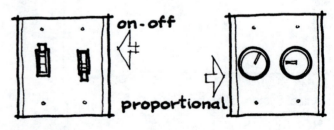

FIGURE 5.23

locity sensors include bellows, diaphragms, and sail switches that move in response to changing pressure or air speed. Humidity sensors often rely on the movement of a human hair although other materials and electrical circuits are also used. Electrical sensors change circuit resistance in response to changing temperature or humidity.

Switches and Signal Media

Switches and signal media convert small sensor movements or currents into larger and more powerful signals that can control large motors or valves. Building air-conditioning systems use compressed air and electrical signal media extensively. Compressed air signals position automatic valves and dampers, while electrical signals are used to control electric motors, compressors, fans, and pumps.

Controlled Devices

Controlled devices can include fan motors, compressors, pumps, valves, and dampers. These devices are essentially the same as their manually operated counterparts but their operation or position can be changed by pneumatic or solenoid actuators in response to signal media commands (see Figure 5.24).

SMART BUILDINGS

Smart buildings use state-of-the-art controls in conjunction with computer programs for precise control of building temperature and humidity under varying internal and external load conditions. Numerous sensors and feedback loops coupled with well-conceived operating programs permit anticipatory control where the building can respond to an approaching cold front by starting boilers and warming circulating water temperatures prior to a building thermostat signal requesting heat. Building control operation is as good as the sensor inputs and the operating program.

An amusing story about the first computer-operated building control system is that the program to minimize peak electrical demand by selective shedding of electrical loads began load shedding by cutting power to the controlling computer!

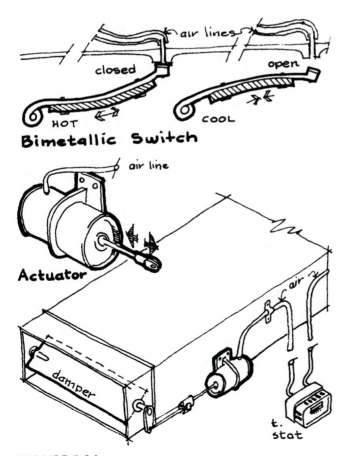

FIGURE 5.24

REVIEW PROBLEMS

A number of problems have been included in the text near the appropriate tables. Solve them first.

1. A small commercial building has a peak heat loss of 300,000 BTUH and a peak heat gain of 240,000 BTUH (heat gain is 180,000 BTUH sensible, and 60,000 BTUH latent). Calculate the CFM that must be distributed by the air handler for heating and cooling. Use 75°F indoor design temperature, 115°F heating air, and 55°F cooling air.

2. Will heating or cooling set the air quantity used to size ducts in problem 1?

3. Calculate cooling CFM again for problem 1 using the rule of thumb value for CFM per ton.

4. Select a round duct to carry 8,000 CFM.

5. Select a rectangular duct to carry 2,500 CFM and fit in a space 14" high. Allow for 1" thick duct insulation.

6. A 24×12 rectangular duct is carrying 2,000 CFM. The duct must split into two branches. One will carry 600 CFM and the other 1,400 CFM. Select branch sizes.

7. Select a rectangular duct to supply 300 CFM to a 10×10 ceiling register.

8. Select a rectangular duct to supply 600 CFM to a 30×8 wall register.

9. Select a ceiling register to deliver 400 CFM with a two-way throw of 10 feet.

10. Select a wall register to deliver 300 CFM with a medium pattern throw of 13 feet.

11. Select a 4' long floor register to deliver 200 CFM in a room with an 8' ceiling height.

12. Select a return air filter grille for a 5-ton air handler.

13. Specify CFM for an exhaust fan that serves a laboratory fume hood. The fume hood inlet opening measures 3'×6' and a minimum inlet air velocity of 50 FPM (feet per minute) is required to ensure safety for lab occupants.

ANSWERS

1. 7,500 CFM for heating, 8,333 CFM for cooling

$$300,000/(1.08)(115-75) = 7,500 \text{ CFM}$$
$$180,000/(1.08)(75-55) = 8,333 \text{ CFM}$$

2. Ducts should be sized to satisfy the larger CFM needed for *cooling*. CFM may be reduced in winter to minimize drafts.

3. 20 tons , 8,000 CFM

$$240,000/12,000 = 20 \text{ tons}, (20)(400) = 8,000$$

Notice that the rule of thumb estimate uses total BTUH (sensible plus latent) instead of the more accurate CFM calculation which uses only the sensible gain taken by conditioned air.

4. Select a 32" diameter airway (plus insulation).

5. Select a 36×10 airway dimension. The outside dimension of the duct will be 38×12. A 32×12 airway duct would require less material, but there would be no clearance for duct support angles or stiffeners.

6. Split — 10×12 = 600 CFM and 18×12 = 1,400 CFM. Hold a constant duct height for a simple transition.

7. Select a 10×7 duct to fit the register. Many ceiling registers are built with round flanges on the register boot. In such cases a short section of flexible round duct is used between the register and the duct.

8. Use a 30×8 duct *if* there is a short distance (4 feet or less) from the main supply duct to the register. If a longer duct run is required select a 14×8 duct and transition to 30×8 at the register.

9. 18×18

10. 6×16

11. 2 1/2″ × 48″

12. Select two at 20×20 because the 5-ton unit will circulate about 2,000 CFM.

13. This question is not specifically covered in the text but a thinking reader will have no trouble working out an answer. Try before you read on. An air velocity of 1 FPM through an inlet opening with an area of 1 sq. ft. will result in an air flow of 1 CFM. Specify a 900 CFM exhaust fan.

$$(\text{FPM})(\text{area}) = \text{CFM} \quad (50)(6 \times 3) = 900 \text{ CFM}$$

CHAPTER

6

Annual Costs

*In my small village
even the flies aren't afraid
to bite a big man.*

Issa

———✦———

This short chapter lets you predict annual utility costs based on heat loss and heat gain calculations. It draws information from the preceding chapters and uses the house and office examples introduced in Chapter 2 to demonstrate annual cost estimates.

Study the example energy and operating cost estimates with patience. When you develop confidence in your ability to evaluate energy-conserving alternatives you are well on the way to becoming a capable analyst of efficient buildings.

Building owners are particularly interested in costs for obvious reasons, and an important responsibility of designers and constructors is owner education concerning life cycle costs.

Lacking other information, building owners will always select the lowest first cost alternative, but informed owners will opt for high-quality equipment if it offers life cycle cost benefits. Competent building professionals select efficient equipment and communicate potential cost advantages to the owner. Proposing a more efficient (and more expensive) cooling tower with the explanation "it's better" will fall on deaf ears, but proposing the same cooling tower because "its added costs will be paid back in less than two years through utility savings" will earn the owner's respect.

Complete the problems at the end of this chapter and then apply these evaluation techniques to your specific building projects. Remember that your recommendations are only as good as the effort that produces them. They will be respected if they are backed with accurate estimates of initial cost and payback.

———✦———

6.0 ESTIMATE ANNUAL ENERGY

Calculated values for heat loss and heat gain may be used to estimate annual energy requirements and costs. The heating and cooling hours maps in Figures 6.1 and 6.2 give estimated full-load operating hours for heating and cooling equipment. Maps are rough estimates; better values can be obtained from local utilities. Do *not* apply map values to buildings that are heated and cooled occasionally, like churches and dance halls, or to buildings that operate 24 hours a day, like hospitals and airline terminals.

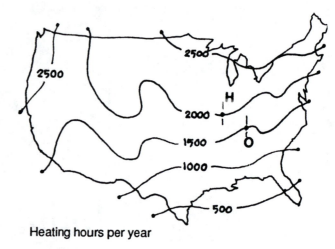

Heating hours per year

FIGURE 6.1

ANNUAL ENERGY

To estimate annual energy requirements in BTU/yr (BTUs per year) multiply the peak heat loss and gain values for a building by the annual full-load heating and cooling hours shown on the maps. Heat loss and gain calculations for the house and office examples developed in Chapter 2 are used again here as the basis of energy and cost estimates.

House

The example house had a calculated peak heat loss of 77,273 BTUH and a peak heat gain of 33,537 BTUH. Estimate annual heating and cooling BTU at location H.

1. The maps show about 2,000 heating hours and 1,000 cooling hours per year at location H.
2. Heating BTU per year: 154,500,000 BTU/yr

   $$(2,000)(77,273) = 154,500,000$$

3. Cooling BTU per year: 33,500,000 BTU/yr

   $$(1,000)(33,537) = 33,500,000$$

Office

The example office building had a calculated peak heat loss of 406,850 BTUH and peak heat gain of 630,172 BTUH. Estimate annual heating and cooling BTU at location O.

1. Maps show about 1,500 hours for heating and cooling at location O.
2. Heating BTU per year: 389,680,000 BTU/yr

   $$(1,500)(406,850) = 610,000,000 \text{ BTU/yr}$$

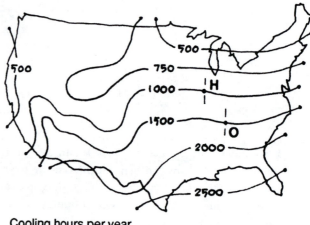

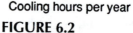
Cooling hours per year

FIGURE 6.2

However, heat contributed by lights* can be credited to total annual heating BTUs.

Lighting heat is 220,320 BTUH. If the heating season lasts 20 weeks, and lights operate 10 hours per day, 5 days per week, they will provide $(220,320)(20)(10)(5) = 220,320,000$ BTU during the heating season. Net office heating BTUs are:

$$610,000,000 - 220,320,000 = 389,680,000$$

3. Cooling BTU per year: 945,000,000 BTU/yr

   $$(1,500)(630,172) = 945,000,000 \text{ BTU/yr}$$

---

*At 3.4 BTU per watt, lights are not efficient heaters, but they do reduce the annual heating load. They also increase the annual cooling load, but that increase is tabulated in the heat gain calculation.

6.1 ESTIMATE ANNUAL ENERGY COSTS

DOLLARS PER YEAR

BTU/yr can be converted to $/yr (dollars per year) if you know the cost of energy and the efficiency of the heating-cooling equipment. The following calculations use the preceding house and office examples with a variety of equipment efficiencies and energy costs. Indoor fan energy is *not* usually included in equipment efficiency ratings, so allow 10% extra for residential air handlers and 20% extra for commercial air handlers with longer duct runs.

Fuel Heat Content	BTU
Coal (anthracite) per lb	14,000
Electricity per kW	3,400
Natural gas per therm (100 CF)	100,000
Natural Gas per MCF (1000 CF)	1,000,000
Oil #2 per gal.	140,000
Propane per gal.	90,000
Wood per lb.	5,000-7,000

Change BTU/yr to $/yr with these equations:

Heating

$$\frac{(\text{BTU/yr})(\$/\text{energy unit})}{(\text{BTU/energy unit})(\text{efficiency})} = \$/\text{yr}$$

Cooling

$$\frac{(\text{BTU/yr})(\$/\text{energy unit})}{(\text{SEER} \times 1,000)} = \$/\text{yr}$$

House: Estimate 1

Heat with oil at $1.00 per gallon and a furnace that is 70% efficient. Cool using an air conditioner with a SEER of 12. Electricity costs $0.10 per kWh (1 gal. oil = 140,000 BTU; SEER 12 = 12,000 BTU/kW).

Heating

$$\frac{(154,500,000)(\$1)}{(140,000)(70\%)} = \$1,577/\text{yr}$$

Cooling

$$\frac{(33,500,000)(\$0.10)}{(12)(1,000)} = \$279/\text{yr}$$

Subtotal $1,856/yr
Add 10% for indoor fan = $2,042/yr

House: Estimate 2

Same example, but use a heat pump with a COP of 2.2 and a SEER of 10 (COP 1 = 3,400 BTU per kW).

Heating

$$\frac{(154,500,000)(\$0.10)}{(3,400)(2.2)} = \$2,066/\text{yr}$$

Cooling

$$\frac{(33,500,000)(\$0.10)}{(10)(1,000)} = \$335/\text{yr}$$

Subtotal $2,401/yr
Add 10% for indoor fan = $2,641/yr

Office: Estimate 1

Heat the office building with natural gas that is 70% efficient at $0.50 per therm. Cool with SEER 10 air conditioners at $0.08 per kWh (1 therm = 100,000 BTU).

Heating

$$\frac{(389,680,000)(\$0.50)}{(100,000)(70\%)} = \$2,783/\text{yr}$$

Cooling

$$\frac{(945,000,000)(\$0.08)}{(10)(1,000)} = \$7,560/\text{yr}$$

Subtotal $10,343/yr
Air handlers add 20% = $12,412/yr

Office: Estimate 2

Same office as Estimate 1 but use heat pumps with a COP of 2.4 and a SEER of 11, electricity at $0.09 per kWh.

Heating

$$\frac{(389,680,000)(\$0.09)}{(3,400)(2.4)} = \$4,298/\text{yr}$$

Cooling

$$\frac{(945,000,000)(\$0.09)}{(11)(1,000)} = \$7,732/\text{yr}$$

Subtotal $12,030/yr
Air handlers add 20% = $14,436/yr
(only a bit more than $1,600 a month)

Cautions! The preceding calculations can provide reasonable first estimates, but precision depends on accurate annual heating and cooling hours. Local electrical utilities and fuel suppliers are the best source of annual heating and cooling hour information for many building types.

The calculations can be applied with some confidence to residential and smaller commercial occupancies. However, they will not apply to 24-hour-a-day occupancies like hospitals and airline terminals, or intermittent occupancies like theaters and churches.

6.2 EVALUATE ENERGY-CONSERVING ALTERNATIVES

Section 6.1 proposed a method for estimating annual heating and cooling costs. The same method may be used to evaluate energy-conserving alternatives.

awesome savings !

Calculations in this section are based on the example office building used in Chapter 2. Alternates 1 through 3 assume 1,600 heating hours and 1,400 cooling hours. Alternates 4 & 5 use 1,500 hours for both heating and cooling.

ALTERNATE 1: SLAB EDGE INSULATION

An insulation contractor proposes to reduce building heat loss by installing slab edge insulation for $2,000 (see Figure 6.3). Evaluate the proposal by estimating the payback period.

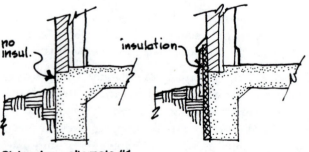

Slab edge - alternate #1

FIGURE 6.3

Given

Slab edge length is 494 linear feet.
The slab edge U value without insulation is 0.8; with insulation U is 0.1.
Winter TD (temperature difference) is 60.
Annual full-load heating hours = 1,600.
Heat is electric resistance at $0.06/kWh (each kWh yields 3,400 BTUH).

Heating Savings

No insulation	(0.8)(494)(60) =	23,712 BTUH
With insulation	(0.1)(494)(60) =	2,964 BTUH
	Peak heat loss saving	20,748 BTUH

First-Year Heating Savings

$$\frac{(20,748)(1,600)(0.06)(1.2)}{3,400} = \$703$$

Summary

Estimated simple payback: 2.8 years.
Payback = 2,000/703 = 2.8 years.

ALTERNATE 2: MORE ROOF INSULATION

The roofing contractor offers to increase the thickness of urethane roof insulation from 3″ to 4″ for $3,000. Evaluate this proposal by estimating the payback period.

Given

Roof area is 10,800 sq. ft.
Roof U value with 3″ urethane is 0.05; U with 4″ urethane is 0.04.
Winter TD is 60°F; summer ETD is 36°F.
Annual full-load heating hours = 1,600.
Heat with an 80% efficient gas furnace with gas at $0.75 per therm.
Annual full-load cooling hours = 1,400.
Cool with SEER-10 air conditioners; electricity costs $0.09 per kWh.

Heating Savings

3″ roof $(0.05)(10,800)(60) = 32,400$ BTUH

4″ roof $(0.04)(10,800)(60) = \underline{25,920 \text{ BTUH}}$

Peak heat loss savings 6,480 BTUH

First-Year Heating Savings

$$\frac{(6,480)(1,600)(\$0.75)(1.2)}{(100,000)(80\%)} = \$116.64/\text{yr}$$

Cooling Savings

3″ roof $(0.05)(10,800)(36) = 19,440$ BTUH

4″ roof $(0.04)(10,800)(36) = \underline{15,552 \text{ BTUH}}$

Peak heat gain savings 3,888 BTUH

First-Year Cooling Savings

$$\frac{(3,888)(1,400)(\$0.09)(1.2)}{(10)(1,000)} = \$58.79/\text{yr}$$

Summary

Estimated simple payback: 17.1 years.
Annual heating and cooling savings is $175.43
    (calculations include 20% for air handlers).
Payback = 3,000/175 = 17.1 years.

ALTERNATE 3: LESS VENTILATION

The HVAC and insulation contractors propose to weatherstrip the building and cut the average ventilation rate to 2,000 CFM. Added costs for controls and weatherstripping will total $2,500.

Given

Original design was 2,970 CFM winter, 2,400 CFM
    summer. New design is 2,000 CFM for both
    winter and summer.
Winter TD is 60°F; summer TD is 20°F.
GD (grain difference) is 40.
Heat with a 75% efficient oil-fired boiler using
    $0.90 per gallon oil.
Annual heating hours = 1,600.
Annual cooling hours = 1,400.
Cool with a SEER-8 (net) electric chiller; electricity
    costs $0.07 per kWh.

Heating Savings

Original: $(2,970)(1.08)(60) = 192,456$ BTUH

Proposal: $(2,000)(1.08)(60) = \underline{129,600 \text{ BTUH}}$

Peak heat-loss savings 62,856 BTUH

First-Year Heating Cost Savings

$$\frac{(62,856)(1,600)(\$0.90)(1.2)}{(140,000)(75\%)} = \$1,034/\text{yr}$$

Cooling Savings

Original sensible: $(2,400)(1.08)(20) = 51,840$ BTUH

Original latent: $(2,400)(0.68)(40) = \underline{65,280 \text{ BTUH}}$

Original total 117,120 BTUH

New sensible: $(2,000)(1.08)(20) = 43,200$ BTUH

New latent: $(2,000)(0.68)(40) = \underline{54,400 \text{ BTUH}}$

New total   97,600 BTUH

Peak cooling saving   19,520 BTUH

First-Year Cooling Cost Savings

$$\frac{(19,520)(1,400)(\$0.07)(1.2)}{(8)(1,000)} = \$287/\text{yr}$$

Total heating and cooling savings $1,321/yr

Summary

Estimated simple payback: 1.9 years.
Payback = 2,500/1,321 = 1.9 years.

Caution! Check the number of building occupants *before* reducing the ventilation rate. In many localities, 15 CFM/occupant is a minimum code requirement.

ALTERNATE 4: IMPROVED HEAT PUMPS

The HVAC subcontractor proposes to furnish more efficient heat pumps for $10,000 extra. Evaluate the proposal by estimating payback.

Given

The specified heat pumps have a COP of 2 and a
    SEER of 9. High-efficiency heat pumps have a
    COP of 2.8 and a SEER of 13.
Electricity costs $0.08/kWh.

Annual heat loss is 389,680,000 BTU per year. Heat gain is 945,000,000 BTU per year.

Note: 1,500 full-load heating and cooling hours are used to calculate BTU per year for this example.

Heating Savings

Specified $\dfrac{(389,680,000)(\$0.08)(1.2)}{(3,400)(2)} = \$5,501/yr$

Efficient $\dfrac{(389,680,000)(\$0.08)(1.2)}{(3,400)(2.8)} = \$3,929/yr$

First-year heating savings $1,572/yr

Cooling Savings

Specified $\dfrac{(945,000,000)(\$0.08)(1.2)}{(9)(1,000)} = \$10,080/yr$

Efficient $\dfrac{(945,000,000)(\$0.08)(1.2)}{(13)(1,000)} = \$6,978/yr$

First-year cooling savings $3,102/yr

Total heating and cooling savings allowing 20% for air handlers $4,674/yr

Summary

Estimated simple payback: 2.1 years.
Payback = 10,000/4,674 = 2.1 years.

ALTERNATE 5: REFLECTIVE WINDOWS*

The glazing contractor proposes to provide reflective windows instead of clear windows for $2,470 extra. Evaluate the proposal by estimating payback.

Given

Glass area totals 2,470 sq. ft.
Shading coefficient (SC) for original glass was 85%; SC for proposed reflective glass is 45%.
Solar factor (SF) is 36 (weighted average for north and shaded south glass).
Annual cooling hours = 1,500.
Cooling SEER is 9; electricity costs $0.12 per kWh.

Heating Savings

None! Reflective glass probably increases winter heating requirements because of reduced solar gain for the south-facing windows. However, the lower emittance of a reflective surface improves the U value of all window areas.

The example estimates *only* summer cooling savings.

Cooling Savings

Original glass: $(36)(2,470)(85\%) = 75,582$ BTUH
Reflective: $(36)(2,470)(45\%) = \underline{40,014}$ BTUH
                  Peak cooling savings 35,568 BTUH

First-Year Cooling Cost Savings

$$\dfrac{(35,568)(1,500)(\$0.12)(1.2)}{(9)(1,000)} = \$854/yr$$

Summary

Estimated simple payback: 2.9 years.
Payback = 2,470/854 = 2.9 years.

---

*Alternate 5 may overestimate annual cooling savings credited to reflective glass because an average solar factor is used. More accurate estimates can be developed using actual solar data for the building site.

REVIEW PROBLEMS

Set up and solve each of the following problems *before* checking your solutions.

1. Evaluate Furnaces

Two furnaces are being considered for a proposed elementary school. Furnace **A** costs $1,200 and has a 75% operating efficiency. Furnace **B** is a condensing type that costs $2,000 and has a 95% operating efficiency. Find the simple payback period for furnace B.

Given:
Furnace capacity = 240,000 BTUH
School peak heat loss = 200,000
Natural gas at $0.60 per therm (100,000 BTU)
Annual full-load heating hours = 1,700

Solution
First find heating BTU per year, then $ per year for each furnace.

BTU per year = (peak heat loss)(full-load hr/yr)
   (200,000)(1,700) = 340,000,000 BTU
$ per yr = (BTU per yr)($ fuel)/(BTU-
   fuel)(efficiency)

Furnace A
$$\frac{(340,000,000)(\$0.60)}{(100,000)(75\%)} = \$2,720$$

Furnace B
$$\frac{(340,000,000)(\$0.60)}{(100,000)(95\%)} = \$2,147$$

Furnace B costs $800 extra and will save $573 in heating costs each year. The simple payback for furnace B is 1.4 years.

2. Evaluate Storm Windows

Storm windows for a residence will cost $500 ($2.50 per sq. ft. of window area). Find the simple payback period for storm windows.

Given:
U value existing windows = 1.1
U value with storm windows added = 0.6
Winter TD = 70°F
Electric heat pump COP = 2.4
Electricity at $0.07 per kWh

Annual full-load heating hours = 1,900
Summer TD = 20°F
Electric heat pump SEER = 10.0
Annual full-load cooling hours = 800

Solution*
Consider just 1 sq. ft. of window area. First calculate heat loss and gain, then convert BTU to $ per year.

Peak Heat Loss = (U)(area)(TD)
   No storm (1.1)(1)(70) = 77 BTUH
   Storm on (0.6)(1)(70) = 42 BTUH
Heat Loss/Year: (BTUH)(full-load hr)
   No storm (77)(1,900) = 146,300 BTU/yr
   Storm on (42)(1,900) = 79,800 BTU/yr
Heating $/Year:
$$\frac{(BTU)(\$ \text{ fuel})}{(BTU\text{-fuel})(\text{efficiency})}$$
   No storm $\dfrac{(146,300)(0.07)}{(3,400)(2.4)} = \$1.26$

   Storm on $\dfrac{(79,800)(0.07)}{(3,400)(2.4)} = \underline{\$0.68}$
   Storm windows save $0.58 per sq. ft.

Peak Heat Gain* = (U)(area)(TD)
   No storm (1.1)(1)(20) = 22 BTUH
   Storm on (0.6)(1)(20) = 12 BTUH
Heat Gain/Year: (BTUH)(full-load hr)
   No storm (22)(800) = 17,600 BTU
   Storm on (12)(800) = 9,600 BTU
Cooling $/Year:
$$\frac{(BTU)(\$ \text{ per kW})}{(SEER)(1,000)}$$
   No storm $\dfrac{(17,600)(0.07)}{(10)(1,000)} = \$0.12$

   Storm on $\dfrac{(9,600)(0.07)}{(10)(1,000)} = \underline{\$0.07}$
   Storm windows save $0.05 per sq. ft.

Sum annual heating and cooling savings per sq. ft. of window area and add 10% for indoor fans:

$$(0.58 + 0.05)(110\%) = \$0.69$$

---

*This solution is incomplete because it ignores solar gain reductions and the probability that infiltration rates will be reduced by storm windows. Use the tables on pages 124–129 to see if summer and winter solar gain changes cancel out. Problem 4 illustrates the procedure for estimating cost savings due to reduced infiltration or ventilation. The difficulty is estimating the infiltration CFM reduction caused by storm windows.

Storm windows cost $2.50 per sq. ft. and they should save $0.69 per sq. ft. in heating and cooling costs. The simple payback is 3.6 years.

3. Evaluate Cooling Equipment

Two 100-ton chillers are being considered for a department store (see Figure 6.4). **Chiller A** costs $44,000 and has a net SEER of 7.1. **Chiller B** costs $50,000 and has a net SEER of 8.6 (net SEER values include chill water pumps, cooling tower pumps and fans, and air handler fans). Find the simple payback period for chiller B.

Given:
Peak heat gain = 1,200,000 BTUH
Electricity at $0.08 per kWh
Annual full-load cooling hours = 1,800

Solution
First find cooling BTU per year, then $ per year for each chiller.

BTU per year = (peak heat gain)(full-load hr/yr)
    (1,200,000)(1,800) = 2,160,000,000 BTU
$ per yr =(BTU per yr)($ per kW) (SEER)(1,000)

Chiller A

$$\frac{(2,160,000,000)(\$0.08)}{(7.1)(1,000)} = \$24,338$$

Chiller B

$$\frac{(2,160,000,000)(\$0.08)}{(8.6)(1,000)} = \$20,093$$

Chiller B savings/yr = $4,245

Chiller B costs $6,000 extra and will save $4,245/yr. The simple payback for chiller B is 1.4 years.

FIGURE 6.4

4. Evaluate Reduced Ventilation

A HVAC engineer recommends a 2,800 CFM reduction of an existing hospital's ventilation rate. The ventilation system maintains positive pressure in most areas so infiltration is not a concern. Find the annual heating and cooling cost savings due to the reduced ventilation rate.

Given:
Winter TD = 66°F
Gas boiler heating at 80% efficiency
Natural gas at $0.60 per therm
Annual full-load heating hours = 1,100
Summer TD = 15°F
Summer GD = 40
Electric chiller, net SEER = 7.2
Electricity at $0.07 per kWh
Annual full-load cooling hours = 2,600

Solution
First find peak BTUH savings, then annual BTU saved, and finally annual $ saved.

Heat Loss Savings BTUH: (CFM)(1.08)(TD)
    (2,800)(1.08)(66) = 199,584 BTUH
Heat Loss Savings BTU/Year: (BTUH)(full-load hours)
    (199,584)(1,100) = 219,542,400 BTU
Heat $/Year Saved:

$$\frac{(BTU)(\$\ fuel)}{(BTU\text{-}fuel)\ (efficiency)}$$
$$\frac{(219,542,400)(\$0.60)}{(100,000)(80\%)} = \$1,647$$

Heat Gain Savings BTUH: (CFM)(1.08)(TD) = sensible, plus (CFM)(0.68)(GD) = latent
Sensible BTUH
    (2,800)(1.08)(15) = 45,360 BTUH
Latent BTUH
    (2,800)(0.68)(40) = 76,160 BTUH
    Total savings BTUH = 121,520 BTUH
Heat Gain Savings BTU/Year: (BTUH)(full-load hours)
    (121,520)(2,600) = 315,952,000 BTU
Cooling $/Year Saved:

$$\frac{(BTU)(\$\ per\ kW)}{(SEER)(1,000)}$$
$$\frac{(315,952,000)(\$0.07)}{(7.2)(1,000)} = \$3,072$$

Total annual savings due to reduced ventilation ($ heating + $ cooling)* is $4,719

---

*No air handler % added—included in *net* SEER.

5. Evaluate Wall Insulation

Wall A is made with 2×4 studs at 16″ centers and includes R-11 fiberglass insulation. It can be built at a cost of $1.00 per sq. ft. of wall area.

Wall B is the same as wall A except 1″ thick, R-5 polystyrene sheathing will be nailed to the studs at a total cost of $1.40 per sq. ft.

Wall C is made with 2×6 studs at 24″ centers and includes R-19 fiberglass insulation. It can be constructed for $1.32 per sq. ft. (see Figure 6.5).

You are to determine the heating and cooling costs associated with each wall and recommend one wall type for a new residence.

Given:

Winter TD = 70°F
Gas furnace heating at 90% efficiency
Natural gas at $0.70 per therm
Annual full-load heating hours = 2,000
Summer ETD = 25°F (weighted average for N, S, E, and W orientations)
Electric air-conditioning SEER = 10.0
Electricity at $0.06 per kWh
Annual full-load cooling hours = 1,000

Solution

Consider just 1 sq. ft. of wall area to keep the numbers small. First calculate U values and heat loss-gain for each wall, then convert BTU to $ per year and finally compare the walls.

U Values
    Wall A 1/11 = 0.09
    Wall B 1/16 = 0.06
    Wall C 1/21 = 0.05
Peak Heat Loss: (U)(A)(TD)
    Wall A (0.09)(1)(70) = 6.3 BTUH
    Wall B (0.06)(1)(70) = 4.2 BTUH
    Wall C (0.05)(1)(70) = 3.5 BTUH

Heat Loss/Year: (BTUH)(full-load hours)
    Wall A (6.3)(2,000) = 12,600 BTU
    Wall B (4.2)(2,000) = 8,400 BTU
    Wall C (3.5)(2,000) = 7,000 BTU
Heating $ /Year: (BTU)($ fuel)/(BTU-fuel)(efficiency)

Wall A $\dfrac{(12,600)(\$0.70)}{(100,000)(90\%)} = \$0.098$

Wall B $\dfrac{(8,400)(\$0.70)}{(100,000)(90\%)} = \$0.065$

Wall C $\dfrac{(7,000)(\$0.70)}{(100,000)(90\%)} = \$0.054$

Peak Heat Gain: (U)(A)(ETD)
    Wall A (0.09)(1)(25) = 2.25 BTUH
    Wall B (0.06)(1)(25) = 1.50 BTUH
    Wall C (0.05)(1)(25) = 1.25 BTUH
Heat Gain/Year: (BTUH)(full-load hr)
    Wall A (2.25)(1,000) = 2,250 BTU
    Wall B (1.50)(1,000) = 1,500 BTU
    Wall C (1.25)(1,000) = 1,250 BTU
Cooling $/Year: (BTU)($ per kW)/(SEER)(1,000)

Wall A $\dfrac{(2,250)(\$0.06)}{(10)(1,000)} = \$0.014$

Wall B $\dfrac{(1,500)(\$0.06)}{(10)(1,000)} = \$0.009$

Wall C $\dfrac{(1,250)(\$0.06)}{(10)(1,000)} = \$0.0075$

Sum annual heating and cooling costs per sq. ft. of wall area and then add 10% to each for indoor fan:

Wall A (0.098 + 0.014)(110%) = $0.123
Wall B (0.065 + 0.09)(110%) = $0.081
Wall C (0.054 + 0.0075)(110%) = $0.068

The costs above are the annual heating-cooling costs per sq. ft. for each wall. Evaluate walls B and C compared to the least first cost wall A.

Wall B costs $0.40 extra and will save $0.042 per year ($0.123 - $0.081). This is a 9.5-year simple payback. Wall C costs $0.32 extra and will save $0.055 per year. This is a 5.8-year simple payback.

Recommend wall C, but explain that other alternatives may offer better payback.

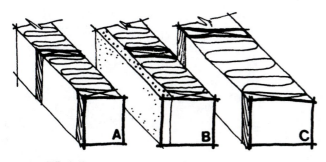

FIGURE 6.5

CHAPTER 7

Efficient Designs

One perfect moon
and the uncountable stars
drowned in a green sky.

Shiki

———◦❀◦———

Contemporary terms include "green" and "sustainable" but whatever the wording, efficiency is an essential ingredient of quality design. Efficient buildings exploit solar, site, and climate opportunities to conserve heating and cooling energy. Talented designers include efficiency as a primary design priority from concept through construction. Efficient buildings don't just happen; they're the result of a continuing commitment by designers, constructors, owners, and operators.

OPPORTUNITIES

Design choices in four areas can reduce building heating and/or cooling costs.

1. **Solar designs.** The winter sun warms south-facing walls. South-facing windows can cut heating costs, and with proper shading they can welcome daylight but exclude direct summer sun.
2. **Thermal mass.** Heavy objects hold heat longer than light objects; earth temperature varies less than air temperature. The earth's thermal mass can be exploited by building underground, and designers can use building mass to delay heat flow.
3. **Evaporation.** In hot-dry climates, evaporative coolers and fountains are economical sources of cool (moist) air.
4. **Air movement.** Increased air velocity can make a warm room comfortable. In some locations, ocean breezes or convective air circulation can replace air-conditioning. Where breezes are few, fans are a bargain compared to air conditioners.

In frigid climates where solar and site factors don't offer comfort opportunities, buildings must be designed to limit heat losses. Minimum surface area and maximum envelope insulation are appropriate design responses for such climates.

———◦❀◦———

7.0 SOLAR DESIGNS

Solar control should be a primary design principle. Buildings that use south-facing windows can enjoy natural heat input during winter months, and summer heat can be excluded with minimal effort. Effective sun control and free winter heating is easy *only for south-facing windows!* Windows that don't face south gain less heat in winter, and shading devices to exclude summer sun are more expensive and less effective. Architectural sun-control surfaces can make a plain building interesting, and an interesting building exciting.

WHY SOUTH-FACING WINDOWS?

Tables 7.1 and 7.2 give the total BTU per sq. ft. per day incident on windows with different orientations during clear winters and summers.

Example

Use Tables 7.1 and 7.2 to estimate the total solar gain through one sq. ft. of south-facing single glass at 40°N during 3 winter months. Assume 60% clear days, 40% cloudy days, for 90 winter days. Use the Nov-Dec-Jan average for clear days and the average north value for cloudy days. Use 90% as the shading coefficient (SC) for clear glass.

Clear days	(54)(1,590)(90%) = 77,274 BTU
Cloudy days	(36)(113)(90%) = 3,661 BTU
	Total solar gain = 80,935 BTU

If the *average* winter temperature difference (TD) across the glass is 30°F, will the glass gain or lose heat during 3 winter months? How much?

Glass heat loss (U)(A)(TD)(total hr) = BTU

(1.1)(1)(30)(90)(24) = 71,280 BTU

One sq. ft. of south-facing window will gain 9,655 BTU over 3 winter months.

SUN CONTROL

Effective shading devices can be designed to admit winter sun and exclude summer sun. For a given latitude (see Figure 7.1) you can easily find the sun's position at any time of the year. *Sun charts* and the *section angle overlay* (in back of this text) indicate the sun's location, and permit you to calculate actual sun lines on

TABLE 7.1

32°N Latitude	N	S	E-W	Hor.
Dec	140	1,700	570	880
Nov or Jan	160	1,690	650	1,020
Oct or Feb	200	1,530	820	1,370
June	520	450	1,170	2,240
May or July	450	500	1,150	2,180
Apr or Aug	330	710	1,090	2,000

TABLE 7.2

40°N Latitude	N	S	E-W	Hor.
Dec	100	1,550	420	560
Nov or Jan	120	1,610	500	700
Oct or Feb	170	1,620	720	1,090
June	500	630	1,230	2,240
May or July	440	700	1,200	2,150
Apr or Aug	310	970	1,090	1,900

building drawings. The charts and overlay will help you set dimensions for shading devices. They are also useful in evaluating daylighting design proposals.

Examples

Use the 30°N sun chart in the following two examples. Sun charts for other latitudes can be found on pp. 110–112.

1. Using *only* the 30°N sun chart find the time and location of sunrise on 21 April.

    Time = 5:30 AM

    Location = 14° north of east

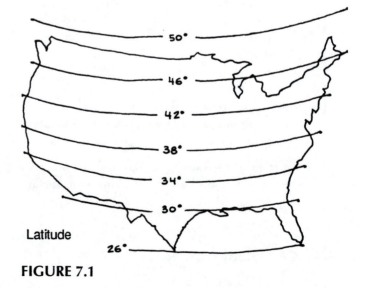

Latitude

FIGURE 7.1

2. Find the sun's bearing (compass direction from observer) at 2 PM on 21 September.

Bearing = 50° west of south

(Extend a line from chart center through the time-date to the bearing ring.)

The following two examples use the 30° sun chart and the **section angle overlay.** Use a pin through the center points of both, and set the "window faces" arrow by rotating the overlay. Read the section angle on the overlay directly above the time-date point on the sun chart.

3. Window faces south. Find the section angle at 3 PM on 21 August.
   Section angle is 75°
4. Window faces 35° west of south. Find the section angle at 3 PM on 21 August.
   Section angle is 50°

Notice that changing the window orientation reduced the section angle. The roof overhang shown in Figure 7.2 excluded direct sun from the south-facing window, but direct sun added to the air-conditioning load for the window facing 35° west of south.

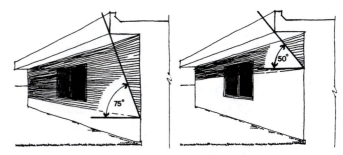

FIGURE 7.2

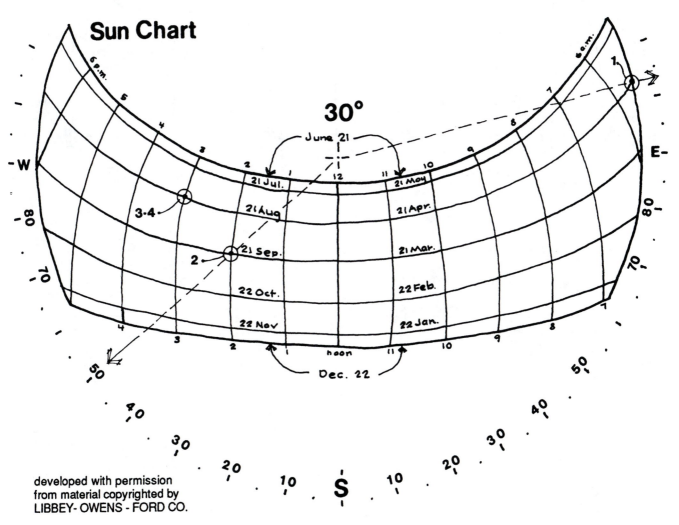

SOLAR DESIGNS

Skillful designers detail windows and shading devices to maximize heat gain during the winter and minimize heat gain during the summer.

Example

Optimize exterior shading for the following window:

1. Window faces south at 30°N latitude.
2. Overheated summer conditions are expected from 21 May through 21 August.
3. Winter heating is required from 22 November through 22 February.

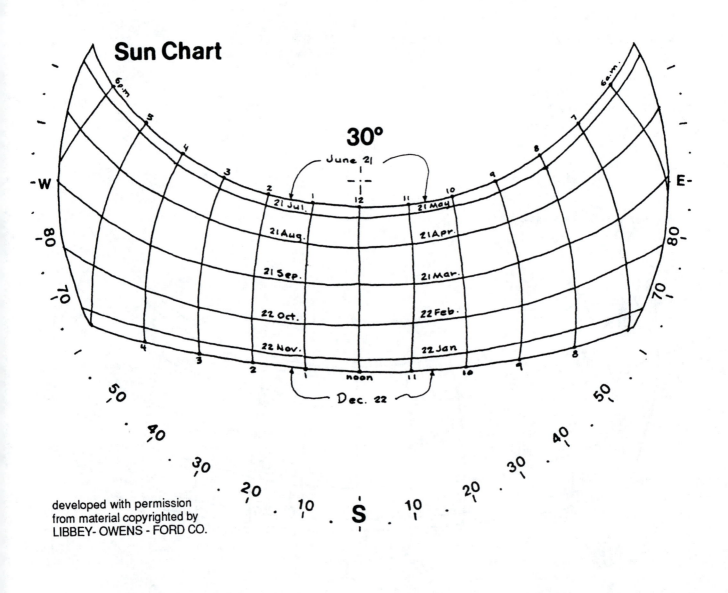

Sun Chart

developed with permission from material copyrighted by LIBBEY- OWENS - FORD CO.

Solution

1. Find the lowest summer section angle using the overlay. Consider summer sun between 7 AM and 5 PM (earlier or later times are not important for south-facing windows because of the sun's bearing).

   70° is the lowest summer section angle (at noon 21 August).

2. Find the highest winter section angle using the overlay. Consider winter sun between 8 AM and 4 PM due to short solar days.

   48° is the highest winter section angle (at noon 22 February). See Figure 7.3.

The optimum shading design shown in Figure 7.4 provides for maximum winter heat gain and minimum summer heat gain.

Repeat the preceding design exercise for a window facing 45° west of south and you will see why south orientation is best. Can you design a shading device for the southwest-facing window? The following trellis example will help if you consider the sun's bearing change from summer to winter.

Example

Design a trellis for a west-facing patio (see Figure 7.5). Exclude direct sun between 4 PM and 7 PM, 21 May through 21 September at 30°N latitude.

Solution

Set the section angle overlay facing due west on the 30° sun chart. Find the highest section angle for the given time-date period.

35° is the highest section angle (at 4 PM on 21 June). Use a 35° angle to space trellis joists.

Talented designers will choose south-facing windows and horizontal shading surfaces at every opportunity. Selected challenges and design details are briefly discussed here.

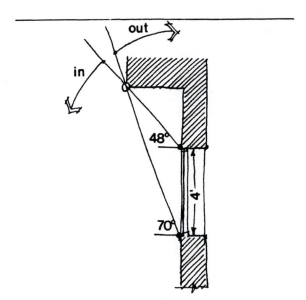

FIGURE 7.4

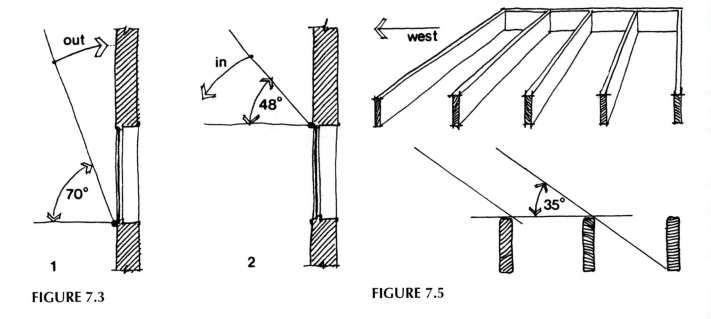

FIGURE 7.3

FIGURE 7.5

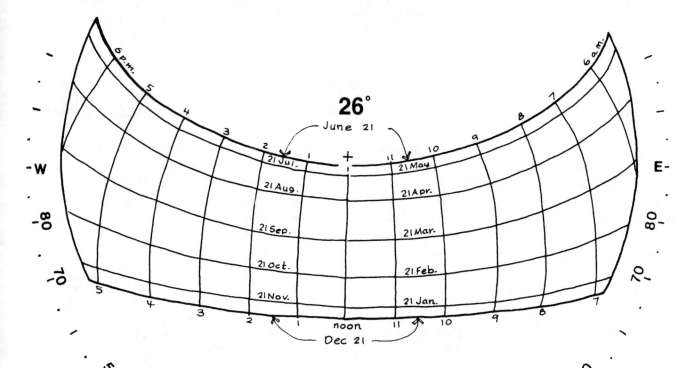

26°

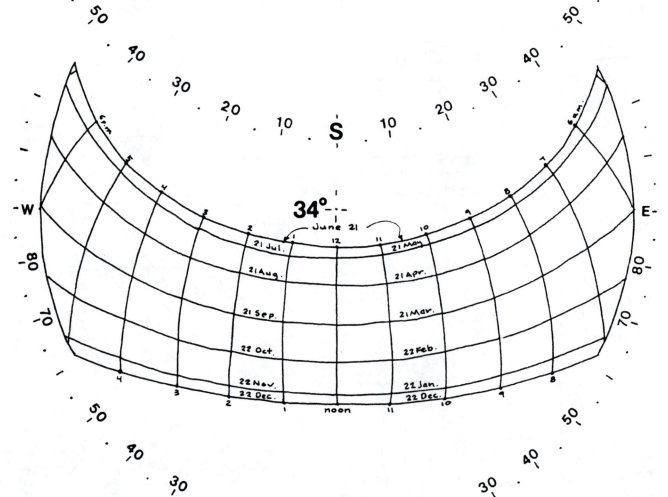

34°

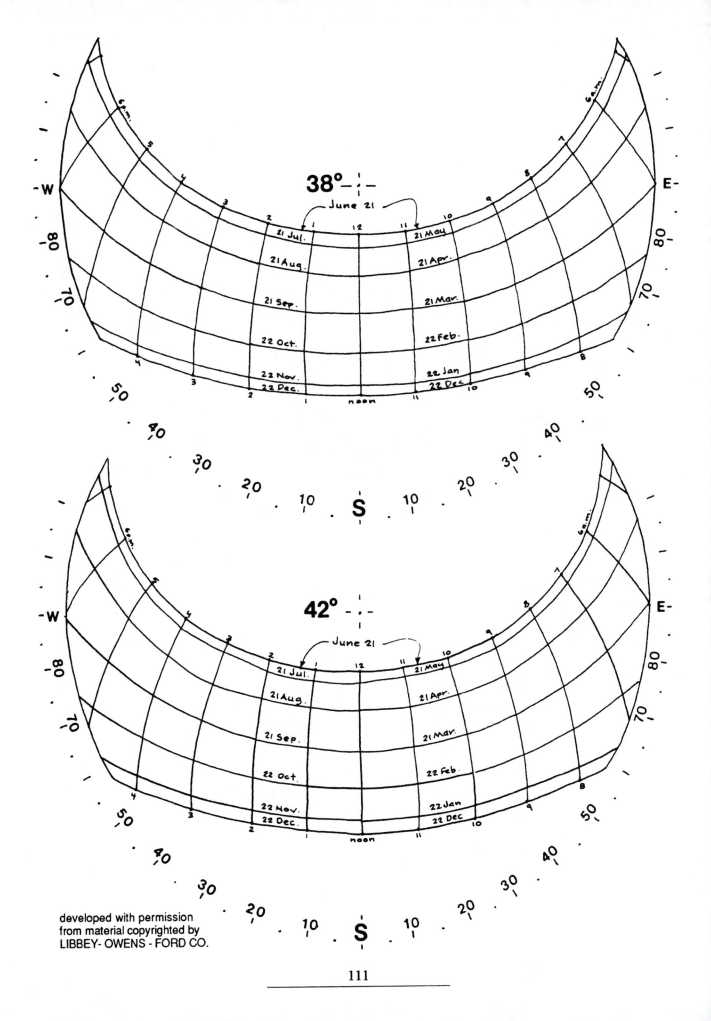

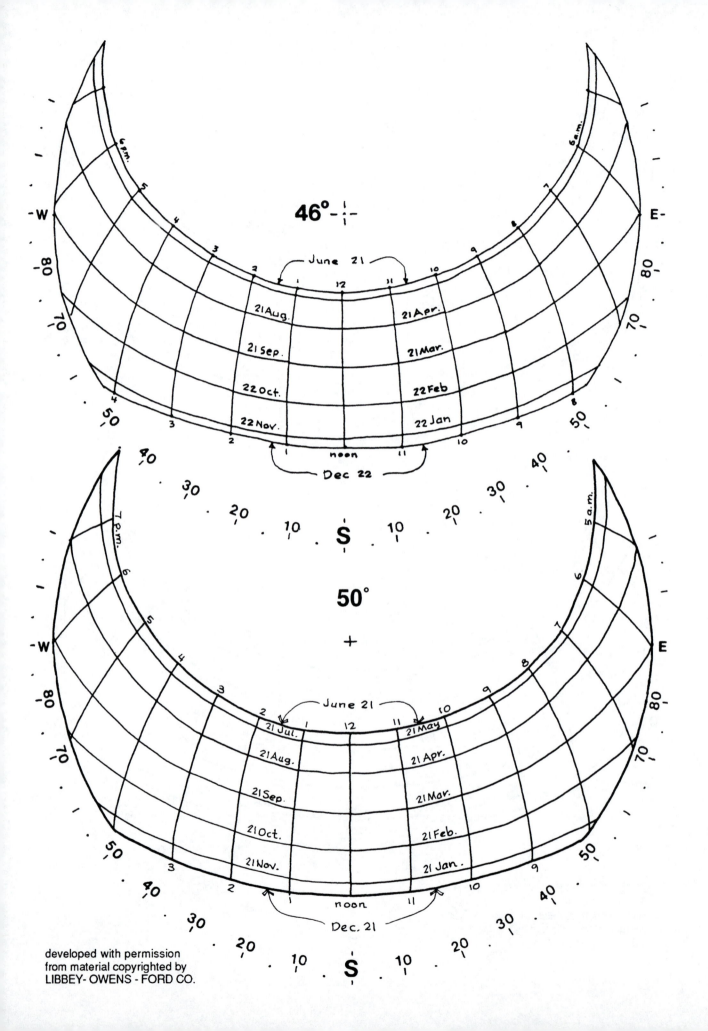

46° -¦-

June 21

21 Aug.   21 Apr.

21 Sep.   21 Mar.

22 Oct.   22 Feb

22 Nov.   22 Jan

noon

Dec 22

W   E

80   80

70   70

50   50

40   30   20   10   S   10   20   30   40

7 p.m.   5 a.m.

50°

+

June 21

21 Jul.   12   11 21 May.

21 Aug.   21 Apr.

21 Sep.   21 Mar.

21 Oct.   21 Feb.

21 Nov.   21 Jan.

noon

Dec. 21

W   E

80   80

70   70

50   50

40   40

30   30

20   10   S   10   20

developed with permission
from material copyrighted by
LIBBEY- OWENS - FORD CO.

SITE CONSTRAINTS

Site orientation, setbacks, and building envelope requirements may suggest window orientations other than south. Imaginative designers orient glass areas facing south even though the building envelope faces otherwise (see Figure 7.6). When interesting views exist at orientations other than south, exploit them with small, carefully shaded glass areas.

SKYLIGHTS

Do *not* use horizontal or sloping roof skylights (see Figure 7.7). They add heat to buildings in summer and leak building heat in winter. Spend a summer day in a greenhouse and you'll be convinced that horizontal glass has no place in buildings. Use clerestories instead (facing south of course). Clerestories eliminate summer overheating and provide winter heat gain. Moveable insulation can minimize night heat losses.

DAYLIGHT

Buildings that exploit daylight use north and south glass. North glass provides the most uniform and diffuse light, but it is a real energy waster in cold climates. South glass offers free heat and maximum light penetration during winter months, but louvers and reflecting surfaces are required to control brightness (see Figure 7.8).

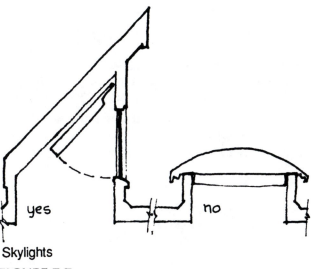

Skylights
FIGURE 7.7

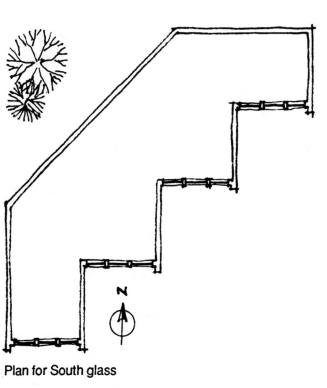

Plan for South glass

FIGURE 7.6

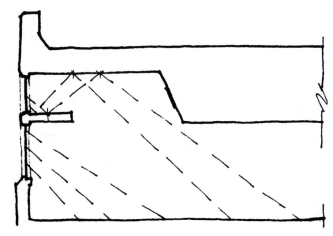

FIGURE 7.8

7.1 THERMAL MASS

UNDERGROUND CONSTRUCTION

Air temperatures at a given location can vary by more than 100°F from summer to winter, but earth temperature several feet below grade will be nearly constant throughout the year (see Figure 7.9). Underground heating and cooling requirements are much lower than for comparable aboveground buildings. The next time a client asks for an energy-efficient home, watch his or her eyes when you suggest an underground structure.

EARTH-SHELTERED CONSTRUCTION

Where underground construction is not practical, south-facing windows plus earth-sheltered designs can provide similar benefits (see Figure 7.10). Careful detailing is required to prevent water and heat leaks where structural members penetrate the earth envelope. Interested? Read *Gentle Architecture* by M. Wells.

MOVEABLE INSULATION

In desert climates, heavy adobe walls can moderate outdoor temperature change. The sun warms adobe walls during the day and they release some heat indoors at night. But adobe walls lose lots of heat to the desert night, and moveable insulation can minimize these losses.

An improved desert design might add exterior moveable insulating panels (see Figure 7.11). In winter months, insulation on the east, south, and west walls would be opened to admit solar energy during the day and closed to retain heat during the night. In the summer, wall and roof insulation would be opened at night to maximize radiant heat loss to the night sky, and closed during the day to keep the interior cool.

Reflective skins on the insulating panels are a further refinement. Interested? Read *Sunspots* by Steve Baer.

FIXED EXTERNAL INSULATION

Insulation on the outside of a building lets interior mass store some heat and delay interior temperature changes. It may save some energy in climates where outdoor conditions fluctuate around a comfortable temperature, but the savings will be small. External insulation is a worthless investment on south-facing walls and in climates where outdoor conditions are uncomfortable for 24 hours each day.

Heat Capacity* of Materials	Volume (cu. ft.)
Insulation (fiberglass, 1 lb/cu. ft.)	150,000
Wood (pine, 32 lb/cu. ft.)	2,400
Rock (gravel up to 3", 100 lb/cu. ft.)	1,250
Concrete (150 lb/cu. ft.)	833
Water (62.4 lb/cu. ft.)	400

*Space required in cubic feet to store 1 million BTU at 40°F above ambient.

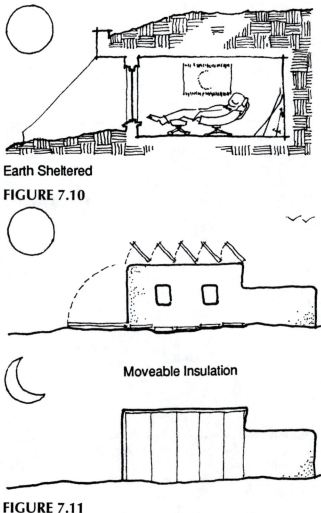

Earth Sheltered

FIGURE 7.10

Moveable Insulation

Underground

FIGURE 7.9

FIGURE 7.11

7.2 EVAPORATION

In air-conditioning equipment a refrigerant evaporates and condenses to move heat. A lot of heat* is absorbed when liquid refrigerant changes to a vapor (evaporates), and this heat is released by the vapor when it condenses.

EVAPORATIVE COOLERS

In dry climates, evaporative coolers can be used instead of air conditioners. They change hot-dry air into cool-moist air and use less than 10 percent of the energy required by a conventional air conditioner.

Unfortunately, evaporative coolers don't work in humid climates; their output is cool air, but its moisture content is too high for comfort. Indirect evaporative coolers can provide *limited* cooling in humid climates because they cool without adding moisture to the building air supply (see Figure 7.12).

COOLING TOWERS

Cooling towers are evaporative coolers used to dump large quantities of heat from generation or refrigeration processes. A perfectly efficient cooling tower would cool water to the wet-bulb temperature of surrounding air, but operating towers usually deliver cooled water at about 10°F above the ambient wet bulb.

Large power plants use convective cooling towers to save fan energy (Figure 7.12).

FOUNTAINS AND TREES

A sheltered courtyard with a fountain is cooler than nearby dry spaces because of evaporation. Fountains can be used for outdoor cooling, or they can replace cooling towers as a means of dumping heat to the environment.

Trees also do a fine job of cooling summer air by transpiration. A depressed seating area under a large tree can be very comfortable on a hot summer day.

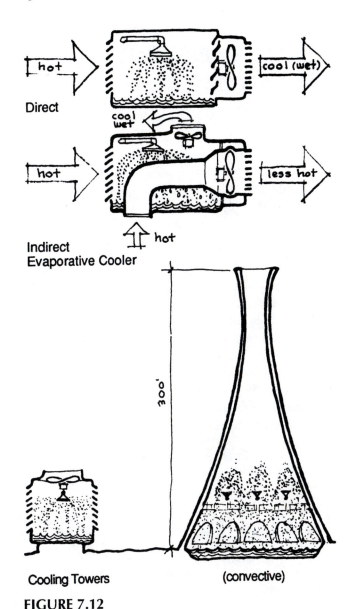

Direct

Indirect Evaporative Cooler

Cooling Towers

(convective)

FIGURE 7.12

---

*"Latent heat of vaporization" is the amount of heat required to change a liquid into a vapor. About 1,000 BTU (1,060) are absorbed when a pound of water becomes a pound of water vapor. These BTU are released when the vapor condenses.

7.3 AIR MOVEMENT

Building air-conditioning equipment is designed to provide gentle air movement at a speed of about 50 feet per minute (FPM) around people. Increased air speed will increase skin heat losses and permit summer comfort at higher air temperatures (see Figure 7.13). At 200 FPM, air temperature can be increased 5°F. At 700 FPM, air temperature can be increased 10°F.

WIND

Wind can induce indoor air circulation. Designs using natural ventilation exploit breezes with large openings high on leeward walls and small openings on the windward walls at occupant level (see Figure 7.14). Small openings can provide a jet effect, increasing air velocity in the occupied zone. Natural ventilation designs are effective where wind direction and speed are fairly constant, but they're useless on sites where wind speed and direction vary a great deal (most locations)!

50 FPM-75°   200 FPM-80°   700 FPM 85°

Velocity - Temperature, relationships

FIGURE 7.13

CONVECTION

Warm air rises, and cool air settles, due to density difference. In winter, upper stories can enjoy a second use of heat that rises from the floor below. In summer, spaces with high ceilings will be cooler than those with low ceilings because the warmest air stratifies above the occupied zone. Summer designs exploit convective heat flow with high outlets and low inlets for occupied spaces (see Figure 7.15).

Convection can also be used to lower summer ceiling temperatures. Continuous eave and ridge vents wash the under side of a hot roof with air which limits heat gain and cuts the ceiling temperature.

FANS

In locations with slow or unpredictable summer winds, fans provide continuous air movement that may substitute for cooling equipment. An exhaust fan that draws outdoor air through a building uses much less energy than an air conditioner.

Summer energy savings are also possible using ceiling fans and higher indoor temperature settings for air-conditioning equipment, but air speeds above 250 FPM in the occupied zone can be disturbing (papers move, pages flutter, etc.).

Winter use of ceiling fans is usually not successful. They bring back warm air from the ceiling but the draft voids the warming effect. Fans can be used in winter to recapture the heat at the ceiling and use it to warm lower floors if moving air is kept outside the occupied zone.

Wind plus convection

FIGURE 7.14

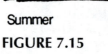

Summer   Winter

FIGURE 7.15

REVIEW PROBLEMS

Solar time is used in all the following review problems. Be sure to adjust solar calculations for your location in a time zone, and for daylight savings time. Solar noon is midway between the sunrise and sunset times usually found in a local newspaper.

1. Size an overhang at the head of a 4-foot-high south-facing window at 42°N latitude to exclude direct sun from 1 June through 21 August.

2. Size an overhang for the window in problem 1 if it is relocated to 30°N latitude.

3. Same window as problem 1 but relocated to 38°N latitude and window faces 30° west of south.

4. Size an exterior vertical shade to exclude direct sun from a window between 3:30 PM and sunset on 21 August. The window is 4 feet high and 3 feet wide. It faces 30° west of south at 38°N latitude.

5. A winery conducts outdoor summer tastings from 4 to 6 PM from 1 June through 31 August. Find the section angle that should be used to space trellis joists above a west-facing tasting area at 42°N latitude.

6. Do horizontal skylights conserve energy?

7. Name the four opportunity areas exploited by efficient building designers; then discuss two example applications of each.

ANSWERS

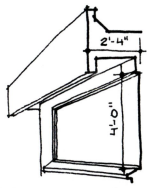

1. The sun is lowest on 21 August at noon when the section angle is about 60°. Use an adjustable triangle or COT 60° to size the overhang.
   (4)(0.58) = 2.3 feet
   COT = cotangent

2. The sun is lowest on 21 August at noon when the section angle is 70°. Use an adjustable triangle or COT 70° to size the overhang.
   (4)(0.33) = 1.32 feet

3. The sun is lowest during the afternoon on 21 August. Section angles are:

   3 PM = 48°
   4 PM = 41°
   5 PM = 32°
   6 PM = 18°

   It is not practical to use an overhang to shade this window. Consider using an overhang equal to the window height which will protect the window from direct sun until about 3:30 PM (section angle 45°). Then add a vertical shade to protect the window from 3:30 PM until sunset.

4. The bearing of the sun at 3:30 PM on 21 August is 75° west of south. After 3:30 PM, bearing shifts toward north. Since the window faces 30° west of south, incident solar rays bear 45° or more to the glass surface. The window is 3 feet wide so specify a vertical shade projecting 3 feet from the west window jamb.

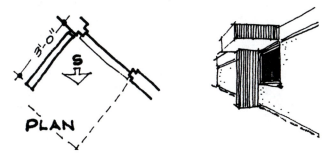

PLAN

5. About 28° is the highest section angle (see p. 111).

6. No! Solar gain is maximum in summer and minimum in winter.

7. Solar control, thermal mass, evaporation, and air movement.

CHAPTER 8

Demand, Solar Heating and First Estimates

*My eyes following
until the bird was lost at sea
found a small island.*

Basho

———◦———

Chapters 1 through 7 developed information to build on as you accept increasing responsibility for the design and construction of efficient buildings. In any field of endeavor there is always more to learn. This final chapter explores two further topics, peak electrical demand and active solar heating.

Peak demand is of interest because it is a significant part of a building's monthly electric bills, and the methods used to cut demand are different from the techniques used to reduce heat gains and losses.

"Active" solar-heating systems use some external energy to collect, store, and move heat. The solar designs in Chapter 7 were "passive." They invited or excluded radiation without help from pumps or fans. On sites where sun is plentiful and electricity is expensive an active solar-heating system may have a reasonable payback. It's a benign energy resource that deserves consideration by designers and builders who have mastered passive solar control.

Finally, this chapter offers "first estimates" that can be helpful before beginning detailed heating and cooling load calculations.

———◦———

8.0 ELECTRICAL PEAK DEMAND

Commercial buildings have two electric meters. One measures consumption in kilowatt hours (kWh) just like a residential meter, but a second meter records peak demand kilowatts (kW) (see Figure 8.1). The demand meter is like an auto speedometer that registers the maximum speed driven, but does not return to zero when the car stops.

Electrical costs for commercial buildings include charges for both consumption and demand. Utilities meter and assess demand charges because they must build and maintain generating capacity that meets their total demand. Generating capacity can be expensive and many utility customers pay more for demand than they pay for energy consumption.

REDUCING COMMERCIAL PEAK

Commercial building designers, constructors, and operators use three methods to reduce demand charges.

1. **Minimize** electrical loads. Efficient buildings are designed and constructed with a continuing commitment to reduce heating, cooling, and lighting loads. Reduced loads and efficient equipment mean less kW demand and lower peak charges.
2. **Delay** electrical loads (thermal storage). Commercial customers can reduce peak demand costs by installing storage capacity, and arranging an off-peak rate with the utility. Laundries can heat and store wash water at night when utility demand is low. Churches can make and store ice with a small refrigeration unit that operates 7 days a week; ice can provide a lot of air-conditioning for a few hours Sunday morning without the peak electrical demand of a large chiller.

   Many utilities provide substantial cash allowances and rate reductions for large commercial customers who install thermal storage equipment.
3. **Sequence** electrical loads. Many refrigeration, heating, pump, and air handler loads can be operated sequentially instead of concurrently. Necessary investments in computers, sensors, and switches can show a 1-year payback from peak demand savings.

REDUCING RESIDENTIAL DEMAND

Most utilities experience system peak demand during hot summer weather, and some are offering cash incentives to builders who reduce residential peak demand (see Figure 8.2). An effective incentive program pays builders a substantial "allowance" for homes with a maximum air-conditioning capacity of 1 ton for each 800 to 1,000 sq. ft. of conditioned area.

Utilities can also limit system demand by installing radio-controlled switches on residential air conditioners or water heaters. Radio signals can shut off a selected group of air conditioners or water heaters for 5 or 10 minutes each hour. Utilities that install this type of equipment enjoy improved system loading and positive peak demand control that can reduce electric costs.

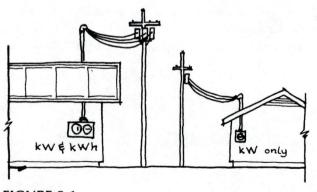

FIGURE 8.1

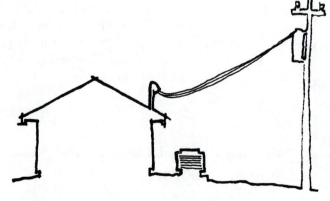

FIGURE 8.2

8.1 SOLAR HEATING

A south-facing window is a passive solar collector. Active solar equipment is distinguished from passive because its operation requires a small amount of non-solar energy. Domestic water heating is the solar application most likely to be cost-effective because hot water is an annual residential need.

ORIENTATION

Solar collectors are positioned to maximize incident insolation.* For maximum annual insolation, collectors are set at an angle equal to the local latitude. To maximize winter insolation, collectors are set at latitude plus 10° (see Figure 8.3).

EFFICIENCY

Solar collectors usually circulate a fluid to absorb energy and store it as heat. Collector efficiency decreases as the temperature of captured heat increases because of losses to the environment. Operating efficiency for solar water-heating equipment can range from 30 to 60%.

---

*Insolation = solar radiation. Verify local values for insolation because the map in Figure 8.4 is very general.

EVALUATION

Consider a solar water heater located in San Francisco. The map in Figure 8.4 indicates each **square foot** of collector will deliver about 600 BTU per day, or 219,000 BTU per year at 40% collector efficiency.

If solar heat is used to replace electric resistance heat at $0.10 per kWh, each square foot of collector can save about $6.44 per year in electric costs.

$$(219,000)($0.10) \div (3,400) = $6.44$$

If solar heat replaces oil at $1.00 per gallon (and 70% heater efficiency), the annual savings per square foot of collector will be about $2.23.

$$(219,000)($1) \div (140,000)(70\%) = $2.23$$

Projected annual savings can be used to evaluate the rate of return for a solar equipment investment.

SIZING

Sizing collectors to do 100% of the heating task is not cost-effective. As a first guess, size a collector to deliver half of the estimated daily heating need.

Example

A family uses 80 gallons of 140° water each day; supply water is 60°. Estimate the solar collector area required for water heating.

Need $(80)(8.33)(140 - 60) = 53,312$ BTU per day.

If the collector will deliver 600 BTU/sq. ft./day, specify a 45 sq. ft. collector.

$$53,312 \div 600 = 89 \text{ sq. ft.}$$

Use one-half or 45 sq. ft.

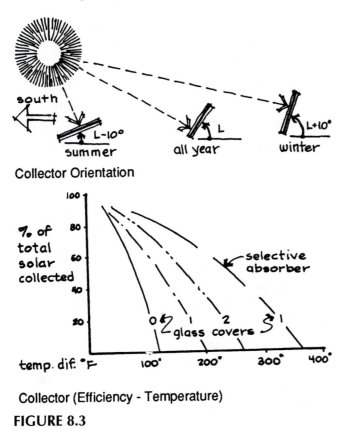

Collector Orientation

Collector (Efficiency - Temperature)

FIGURE 8.3

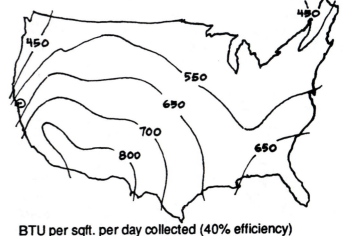

BTU per sqft. per day collected (40% efficiency)

FIGURE 8.4

8.2 FIRST ESTIMATES

These estimates are as good as the individuals who use them. Applied with perception and understanding, they can be an excellent starting point for HVAC estimates and projections, but used without comprehension they will embarrass. Values given are for average or typical practice. Capable designers can achieve substantially better results.

HEATING

For residential or commercial buildings in the United States, estimate peak heating loads at 20 to 60 BTUH per square foot of heated area. Use lower values in southern locations and higher values in northern locations.

Example: Estimate the heating capacity required for a 2,000 sq. ft. home in Miami.

$$(2,000)(20) = 40,000 \text{ BTUH}$$

Example: Estimate required heating capacity for a 20,000 sq. ft. office building in Minneapolis.

$$(20,000)(60) = 1,200,000 \text{ BTUH}$$

Commercial buildings often require less winter heating than residences due to the extra internal heat they receive from lights and occupants; however, they usually need as much peak capacity as a residence to warm up Monday morning after a cold weekend.

COOLING

The range for building peak cooling loads is from 15 to 60 BTUH per square foot of conditioned area. Load variations for air-conditioning are more sensitive to occupancy and internal heat than building location. The cooling season is shorter in Minnesota than in Florida, but a hot day can be as bad in the North as the South. Estimate peak load by building type as follows:

Building Type	Cooling BTUH per sq. ft.
Apartment	15–20
Residence	20–25
School or office	25–35
Retail (furniture or carpet)	25–30
Retail (department store)	30–35
Restaurant	40–50
Hospital	50–60
Dance hall	50–60
Supermarket (why so low?)	10

Exception! For theaters or churches where most of the cooling load is caused by people, just estimate 800 BTUH per seat (range is 600 to 1,000).

Example: Estimate the peak cooling load for a 40,000 sq. ft. school.

$$(40,000)(30) = 1,200,000 \text{ BTUH or 100 tons}$$

Example: Estimate peak cooling load for a 112-seat movie theater.

$$(112)(800) = 89,600 \text{ BTUH or 7.5 tons}$$

AIR QUANTITY

Building cooling load usually determines the total amount of air carried by the duct system. Air quantity ranges from 300 to 500 CFM per ton depending on the proportion of sensible and latent load (higher sensible = higher CFM). Use 400 CFM per ton as a first estimate.

Example: Find air quantity for a 20-ton cooling load.

$$(20)(400) = 8,000 \text{ CFM}$$

MAIN DUCT SIZE

Low-velocity air handlers use air speeds of 1,500 to 2,000 FPM in main ducts. To estimate main duct size, divide CFM by FPM.

Example: Find the main duct size for a 20-ton installation approximately 1,500 FPM.

$$8,000 \div 1,500 = 5.33 \text{ square feet}$$

The duct could be 16"×48"; don't forget that duct insulation will increase overall dimensions. With 1" insulation this duct will be 18"×50".

ELECTRICAL REQUIREMENTS

One horsepower (hp) requires about 1 kW (actually 746 watts at 100% efficiency).

Fans
Exhaust, not ducted	10,000 CFM/hp
Air handler, low velocity	0.3* hp/ton
Air handler, high velocity	Up to 1 hp/ton

AC and Heat Pumps
Air-cooled AC or heat pump	1 kW/ton
Chiller	0.6 to 1 kW/ton

Cooling Tower
Minimum (pump and fan)	0.5kW/ton

*Residential air handlers have much less hp per ton.

WATER QUANTITY

Heating—hot water supply to air handler
(hot water at 20°F TD) 1 gpm carries 10,000 BTUH
Cooling—chill water supply to air handler
(chill water at 10°F TD)   3 gpm/ton

Cooling tower (10°F TD)	3 gpm/ton
Cooling tower make up water	6 gal/ton hour
Water source/sink heat pumps	3 gpm/ton

REFERENCES

Read the following sources for a more comprehensive coverage of energy, design, and HVAC topics.

Energy

Cook, Earl. *Man, Energy, Society.* W.H. Freeman, San Francisco, CA, 1976. *Thoughtful analysis of energy resources and end use efficiency.*

Daniels, Farrington. *Direct Use of the Sun's Energy.* Yale University Press, New Haven, CT, 1964 (also Ballantine Books, NY, 1974). *Explicit coverage of most solar topics.*

Design

Baer, Steve. *Sunspots.* Cloudburst Press, Seattle, WA, 1979. *Solar design, moveable insulation, thermal storage.*

Brown, Reynolds, Ubbelohde. *Insideout.* John Wiley & Sons, New York, NY, 1985. *Solar design workbook.*

Olgyay, Victor. *Design with Climate.* Princeton University Press, Princeton, NJ, 1963. *Passive design.*

Wells, Malcolm. *Gentle Architecture.* McGraw Hill, New York, NY, 1981. *Earth-sheltered construction.*

HVAC

Air Conditioning and Refrigeration Institute. *Refrigeration and Air-Conditioning.* Prentice Hall, Upper Saddle River, NJ, 1979.

Ambrose, E.R. *Heat Pumps and Electric Heating.* John Wiley & Sons, New York, NY, 1966.

ASHRAE Handbook Series; *1997 Fundamentals,* and current *Systems and Applications.* American Society of Heating, Refrigeration, and Air-Conditioning Engineers Inc., Atlanta, GA, 1997.

Egan, M. David. *Concepts in Thermal Comfort.* Prentice Hall, Upper Saddle River, NJ, 1975.

HVAC Plus

Lewis, Jack. *Support Systems for Buildings.* Prentice Hall, Upper Saddle River, NJ, 1986.

Benjamin Stein and John S. Reynolds. *Mechanical and Electrical Equipment for Buildings.* John Wiley & Sons, New York, NY, 1992.

William K. Y. Tao and Richard R. Janis. *Mechanical and Electrical Systems in Buildings.* Prentice Hall, Upper Saddle River, NJ, 1997.

More?

This text emphasizes fundamental HVAC subject matter. Many interesting related topics have been omitted. The following list is a good starting point for readers interested in "alternate" building heating-cooling approaches.

Desiccant cooling
Fuel cell
Heat pipe
Hilsch tube
Indirect evaporative cooling
Piezoelectric heating-cooling
"Rovac" refrigeration
Solar cell
Solar pond
Thermionics

ASHRAE R Value Tables

The following pages of R value information are reprinted by permission of the American Society of Heating, Refrigerating and Air-Conditioning Engineers, Atlanta, Georgia, from the 1997 *ASHRAE Handbook—Fundamentals.*

Publications of the American Society of Heating, Refrigeration, and Air-Conditioning Engineers Inc. are primary HVAC topic references.

Table 1 Surface Conductances and Resistances for Air

Position of Surface	Direction of Heat Flow	Non-reflective $\varepsilon = 0.90$		Reflective $\varepsilon = 0.20$		$\varepsilon = 0.05$	
		h_i	R	h_i	R	h_i	R
STILL AIR							
Horizontal	Upward	1.63	0.61	0.91	1.10	0.76	1.32
Sloping—45°	Upward	1.60	0.62	0.88	1.14	0.73	1.37
Vertical	Horizontal	1.46	0.68	0.74	1.35	0.59	1.70
Sloping—45°	Downward	1.32	0.76	0.60	1.67	0.45	2.22
Horizontal	Downward	1.08	0.92	0.37	2.70	0.22	4.55
MOVING AIR (Any position)		h_o	R				
15-mph Wind (for winter)	Any	6.00	0.17	—	—	—	—
7.5-mph Wind (for summer)	Any	4.00	0.25	—	—	—	—

Notes:
1. Surface conductance h_i and h_o measured in Btu/h·ft²·°F; resistance R in °F·ft²·h/Btu.
2. No surface has both an air space resistance value and a surface resistance value.
3. For ventilated attics or spaces above ceilings under summer conditions (heat flow down), see Table 5.
4. Conductances are for surfaces of the stated emittance facing virtual blackbody surroundings at the same temperature as the ambient air. Values are based on a surface-air temperature difference of 10°F and for surface temperatures of 70°F.
5. See Chapter 3 for more detailed information, especially Tables 5 and 6, and see Figure 1 for additional data.
6. Condensate can have a significant impact on surface emittance (see Table 2).

Table 2 Emittance Values of Various Surfaces and Effective Emittances of Air Spaces[a]

Surface	Average Emittance ε	Effective Emittance ε_{eff} of Air Space	
		One Surface Emittance ε; Other, 0.9	Both Surfaces Emittance ε
Aluminum foil, bright	0.05	0.05	0.03
Aluminum foil, with condensate just visible (> 0.7 gr/ft²)	0.30[b]	0.29	—
Aluminum foil, with condensate clearly visible (> 2.9 gr/ft²)	0.70[b]	0.65	—
Aluminum sheet	0.12	0.12	0.06
Aluminum coated paper, polished	0.20	0.20	0.11
Steel, galvanized, bright	0.25	0.24	0.15
Aluminum paint	0.50	0.47	0.35
Building materials: wood, paper, masonry, nonmetallic paints	0.90	0.82	0.82
Regular glass	0.84	0.77	0.72

[a]These values apply in the 4 to 40 μm range of the electromagnetic spectrum.
[b]Values are based on data presented by Bassett and Trethowen (1984).

these insulation systems (Hooper and Moroz 1952). Deterioration results from contact with several types of solutions, either acidic or basic (e.g., wet cement mortar or the preservatives found in decay-resistant lumber). Polluted environments may cause rapid and severe material degradation. However, site inspections show a predominance of well-preserved installations and only a small number of cases in which rapid and severe deterioration has occurred. An extensive review of the reflective building insulation system performance literature is provided by Goss and Miller (1989).

CALCULATING OVERALL THERMAL RESISTANCES

Relatively small, highly conductive elements in an insulating layer called thermal bridges can substantially reduce the average thermal resistance of a component. Examples include wood and metal studs in frame walls, concrete webs in concrete masonry walls, and metal ties or other elements in insulated wall panels. The following examples illustrate the calculation of R-values and U-factors for components containing thermal bridges.

These conditions are assumed in calculating the design R-values:

- Equilibrium or steady-state heat transfer, disregarding effects of thermal storage
- Surrounding surfaces at ambient air temperature
- Exterior wind velocity of 15 mph for winter (surface with $R = 0.17$°F·ft²·h/Btu) and 7.5 mph for summer (surface with $R = 0.25$°F·ft²·h/Btu)
- Surface emittance of ordinary building materials is 0.90

Wood Frame Walls

The average overall R-values and U-factors of wood frame walls can be calculated by assuming either parallel heat flow paths through areas with different thermal resistances or by assuming isothermal planes. Equations (1) through (5) from Chapter 22 are used.

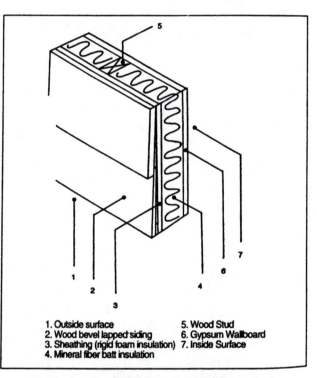

1. Outside surface
2. Wood bevel lapped siding
3. Sheathing (rigid foam insulation)
4. Mineral fiber batt insulation
5. Wood Stud
6. Gypsum Wallboard
7. Inside Surface

Fig. 2 Insulated Wood Frame Wall (Example 1)

The framing factor or fraction of the building component that is framing depends on the specific type of construction, and it may vary based on local construction practices—even for the same type of construction. For stud walls 16 in. on center (OC), the fraction of insulated cavity may be as low as 0.75, where the fraction of studs, plates, and sills is 0.21 and the fraction of headers is 0.04. For studs 24 in. OC, the respective values are 0.78, 0.18, and 0.04. These fractions contain an allowance for multiple studs, plates, sills, extra framing around windows, headers, and band joists. These assumed framing fractions are used in the following example, to illustrate the importance of including the effect of framing in determining the overall thermal conductance of a building. The actual framing fraction should be calculated for each specific construction.

Table 4 Typical Thermal Properties of Common Building and Insulating Materials—Design Values[a]

Description	Density, lb/ft³	Conductivity[b] (k), Btu·in h·ft²·°F	Conductance (C), Btu h·ft²·°F	Resistance[c] (R) Per Inch Thickness (1/k), °F·ft²·h Btu·in	Resistance[c] (R) For Thickness Listed (1/C), °F·ft²·h Btu	Specific Heat, Btu lb·°F
BUILDING BOARD						
Asbestos-cement board	120	4.0	—	0.25	—	0.24
Asbestos-cement board ....0.125 in.	120	—	33.00	—	0.03	
Asbestos-cement board ....0.25 in.	120	—	16.50	—	0.06	
Gypsum or plaster board ....0.375 in.	50	—	3.10	—	0.32	0.26
Gypsum or plaster board ....0.5 in.	50	—	2.22	—	0.45	
Gypsum or plaster board ....0.625 in.	50	—	1.78	—	0.56	
Plywood (Douglas Fir)[d]	34	0.80	—	1.25	—	0.29
Plywood (Douglas Fir).................................0.25 in.	34	—	3.20	—	0.31	
Plywood (Douglas Fir).................................0.375 in.	34	—	2.13	—	0.47	
Plywood (Douglas Fir).................................0.5 in.	34	—	1.60	—	0.62	
Plywood (Douglas Fir).................................0.625 in.	34	—	1.29	—	0.77	
Plywood or wood panels.............................0.75 in.	34	—	1.07	—	0.93	0.29
Vegetable fiber board						
Sheathing, regular density[c] ....0.5 in.	18	—	0.76	—	1.32	0.31
....0.78125 in.	18	—	0.49	—	2.06	
Sheathing intermediate density[c].................0.5 in.	22	—	0.92	—	1.09	0.31
Nail-base sheathing[c] ....0.5 in.	25	—	0.94	—	1.06	0.31
Shingle backer................................0.375 in.	18	—	1.06	—	0.94	0.31
Shingle backer................................0.3125 in.	18	—	1.28	—	0.78	
Sound deadening board........................0.5 in.	15	—	0.74	—	1.35	0.30
Tile and lay-in panels, plain or acoustic	18	0.40	—	2.50	—	0.14
....0.5 in.	18	—	0.80	—	1.25	
....0.75 in.	18	—	0.53	—	1.89	
Laminated paperboard	30	0.50	—	2.00	—	0.33
Homogeneous board from repulped paper....	30	0.50	—	2.00	—	0.28
Hardboard[e]						
Medium density	50	0.73	—	1.37	—	0.31
High density, service-tempered grade and service						
grade..	55	0.82	—	1.22	—	0.32
High density, standard-tempered grade	63	1.00	—	1.00	—	0.32
Particleboard[e]						
Low density..	37	0.71	—	1.41	—	0.31
Medium density	50	0.94	—	1.06	—	0.31
High density...	62	.5	1.18	—	0.85	—
Underlayment.................................0.625 in.	40	—	1.22	—	0.82	0.29
Waferboard	37	0.63	—	1.59	—	—
Wood subfloor ....0.75 in.	—	—	1.06	—	0.94	0.33
BUILDING MEMBRANE						
Vapor—permeable felt................................	—	—	16.70	—	0.06	
Vapor—seal, 2 layers of mopped 15-lb felt.................	—	—	8.35	—	0.12	
Vapor—seal, plastic film	—	—	—	—	Negl.	
FINISH FLOORING MATERIALS						
Carpet and fibrous pad	—	—	0.48	—	2.08	0.34
Carpet and rubber pad....................................	—	—	0.81	—	1.23	0.33
Cork tile ....0.125 in.	—	—	3.60	—	0.28	0.48
Terrazzo ....1 in.	—	—	12.50	—	0.08	0.19
Tile—asphalt, linoleum, vinyl, rubber..........................	—	—	20.00	—	0.05	0.30
vinyl asbestos................................						0.24
ceramic......................................						0.19
Wood, hardwood finish....................0.75 in.	—	—	1.47	—	0.68	
INSULATING MATERIALS						
Blanket and Batt[f,g]						
Mineral fiber, fibrous form processed						
from rock, slag, or glass						
approx. 3-4 in.	0.4-2.0	—	0.091	—	11	
approx. 3.5 in.	0.4-2.0	—	0.077	—	13	
approx. 3.5 in.	1.2-1.6	—	0.067	—	15	
approx. 5.5-6.5 in.	0.4-2.0	—	0.053	—	19	
approx. 5.5 in.	0.6-1.0	—	0.048	—	21	
approx. 6-7.5 in.	0.4-2.0	—	0.045	—	22	
approx. 8.25-10 in.	0.4-2.0	—	0.033	—	30	
approx. 10-13 in.	0.4-2.0	—	0.026	—	38	
Board and Slabs						
Cellular glass..	8.0	0.33	—	3.03	—	0.18
Glass fiber, organic bonded	4.0-9.0	0.25	—	4.00	—	0.23
Expanded perlite, organic bonded......................	1.0	0.36	—	2.78	—	0.30
Expanded rubber (rigid)...............................	4.5	0.22	—	4.55	—	0.40
Expanded polystyrene, extruded (smooth skin surface)						
(CFC-12 exp.)	1.8-3.5	0.20	—	5.00	—	0.29

Table 3 Thermal Resistances of Plane Air Spaces[a,b,c], °F·ft²·h/Btu

Position of Air Space	Direction of Heat Flow	Mean Temp.[d], °F	Temp. Diff.[d], °F	0.5-in. Air Space[c] Effective Emittance ε_{eff}[d,e] 0.03	0.05	0.2	0.5	0.82	0.75-in. Air Space[c] Effective Emittance ε_{eff}[d,e] 0.03	0.05	0.2	0.5	0.82
Horiz.	Up	90	10	2.13	2.03	1.51	0.99	0.73	2.34	2.22	1.61	1.04	0.75
		50	30	1.62	1.57	1.29	0.96	0.75	1.71	1.66	1.35	0.99	0.77
		50	10	2.13	2.05	1.60	1.11	0.84	2.30	2.21	1.70	1.16	0.87
		0	20	1.73	1.70	1.45	1.12	0.91	1.83	1.79	1.52	1.16	0.93
		0	10	2.10	2.04	1.70	1.27	1.00	2.23	2.16	1.78	1.31	1.02
		−50	20	1.69	1.66	1.49	1.23	1.04	1.77	1.74	1.55	1.27	1.07
		−50	10	2.04	2.00	1.75	1.40	1.16	2.16	2.11	1.84	1.46	1.20
45° Slope	Up	90	10	2.44	2.31	1.65	1.06	0.76	2.96	2.78	1.88	1.15	0.81
		50	30	2.06	1.98	1.56	1.10	0.83	1.99	1.92	1.52	1.08	0.82
		50	10	2.55	2.44	1.83	1.22	0.90	2.90	2.75	2.00	1.29	0.94
		0	20	2.20	2.14	1.76	1.30	1.02	2.13	2.07	1.72	1.28	1.00
		0	10	2.63	2.54	2.03	1.44	1.10	2.72	2.62	2.08	1.47	1.12
		−50	20	2.08	2.04	1.78	1.42	1.17	2.05	2.01	1.76	1.41	1.16
		−50	10	2.62	2.56	2.17	1.66	1.33	2.53	2.47	2.10	1.62	1.30
Vertical	Horiz.	90	10	2.47	2.34	1.67	1.06	0.77	3.50	3.24	2.08	1.22	0.84
		50	30	2.57	2.46	1.84	1.23	0.90	2.91	2.77	2.01	1.30	0.94
		50	10	2.66	2.54	1.88	1.24	0.91	3.70	3.46	2.35	1.43	1.01
		0	20	2.82	2.72	2.14	1.50	1.13	3.14	3.02	2.32	1.58	1.18
		0	10	2.93	2.82	2.20	1.53	1.15	3.77	3.59	2.64	1.73	1.26
		−50	20	2.90	2.82	2.35	1.76	1.39	2.90	2.83	2.36	1.77	1.39
		−50	10	3.20	3.10	2.54	1.87	1.46	3.72	3.60	2.87	2.04	1.56
45° Slope	Down	90	10	2.48	2.34	1.67	1.06	0.77	3.53	3.27	2.10	1.22	0.84
		50	30	2.64	2.52	1.87	1.24	0.91	3.43	3.23	2.24	1.39	0.99
		50	10	2.67	2.55	1.89	1.25	0.92	3.81	3.57	2.40	1.45	1.02
		0	20	2.91	2.80	2.19	1.52	1.15	3.75	3.57	2.63	1.72	1.26
		0	10	2.94	2.83	2.21	1.53	1.15	4.12	3.91	2.81	1.80	1.30
		−50	20	3.16	3.07	2.52	1.86	1.45	3.78	3.65	2.90	2.05	1.57
		−50	10	3.26	3.16	2.58	1.89	1.47	4.35	4.18	3.22	2.21	1.66
Horiz.	Down	90	10	2.48	2.34	1.67	1.06	0.77	3.55	3.29	2.10	1.22	0.85
		50	30	2.66	2.54	1.88	1.24	0.91	3.77	3.52	2.38	1.44	1.02
		50	10	2.67	2.55	1.89	1.25	0.92	3.84	3.59	2.41	1.45	1.02
		0	20	2.94	2.83	2.20	1.53	1.15	4.18	3.96	2.83	1.81	1.30
		0	10	2.96	2.85	2.22	1.53	1.16	4.25	4.02	2.87	1.82	1.31
		−50	20	3.25	3.15	2.58	1.89	1.47	4.60	4.41	3.36	2.28	1.69
		−50	10	3.28	3.18	2.60	1.90	1.47	4.71	4.51	3.42	2.30	1.71

Position of Air Space	Direction of Heat Flow	Mean Temp.	Temp. Diff.	1.5-in. Air Space[c] 0.03	0.05	0.2	0.5	0.82	3.5-in. Air Space[c] 0.03	0.05	0.2	0.5	0.82
Horiz.	Up	90	10	2.55	2.41	1.71	1.08	0.77	2.84	2.66	1.83	1.13	0.80
		50	30	1.87	1.81	1.45	1.04	0.80	2.09	2.01	1.58	1.10	0.84
		50	10	2.50	2.40	1.81	1.21	0.89	2.80	2.66	1.95	1.28	0.93
		0	20	2.01	1.95	1.63	1.23	0.97	2.25	2.18	1.79	1.32	1.03
		0	10	2.43	2.35	1.90	1.38	1.06	2.71	2.62	2.07	1.47	1.12
		−50	20	1.94	1.91	1.68	1.36	1.13	2.19	2.14	1.86	1.47	1.20
		−50	10	2.37	2.31	1.99	1.55	1.26	2.65	2.58	2.18	1.67	1.33
45° Slope	Up	90	10	2.92	2.73	1.86	1.14	0.80	3.18	2.96	1.97	1.18	0.82
		50	30	2.14	2.06	1.61	1.12	0.84	2.26	2.17	1.67	1.15	0.86
		50	10	2.88	2.74	1.99	1.29	0.94	3.12	2.95	2.10	1.34	0.96
		0	20	2.30	2.23	1.82	1.34	1.04	2.42	2.35	1.90	1.38	1.06
		0	10	2.79	2.69	2.12	1.49	1.13	2.98	2.87	2.23	1.54	1.16
		−50	20	2.22	2.17	1.88	1.49	1.21	2.34	2.29	1.97	1.54	1.25
		−50	10	2.71	2.64	2.23	1.69	1.35	2.87	2.79	2.33	1.75	1.39
Vertical	Horiz.	90	10	3.99	3.66	2.25	1.27	0.87	3.69	3.40	2.15	1.24	0.85
		50	30	2.58	2.46	1.84	1.23	0.90	2.67	2.55	1.89	1.25	0.91
		50	10	3.79	3.55	2.39	1.45	1.02	3.63	3.40	2.32	1.42	1.01
		0	20	2.76	2.66	2.10	1.48	1.12	2.88	2.78	2.17	1.51	1.14
		0	10	3.51	3.35	2.51	1.67	1.23	3.49	3.33	2.50	1.67	1.23
		−50	20	2.64	2.58	2.18	1.66	1.33	2.82	2.75	2.30	1.73	1.37
		−50	10	3.31	3.21	2.62	1.91	1.48	3.40	3.30	2.67	1.94	1.50
45° Slope	Down	90	10	5.07	4.55	2.56	1.36	0.91	4.81	4.33	2.49	1.34	0.90
		50	30	3.58	3.36	2.31	1.42	1.00	3.51	3.30	2.28	1.40	1.00
		50	10	5.10	4.66	2.85	1.60	1.09	4.74	4.36	2.73	1.57	1.08
		0	20	3.85	3.66	2.68	1.74	1.27	3.81	3.63	2.66	1.74	1.27
		0	10	4.92	4.62	3.16	1.94	1.37	4.59	4.32	3.02	1.88	1.34
		−50	20	3.62	3.50	2.80	2.01	1.54	3.77	3.64	2.90	2.05	1.57
		−50	10	4.67	4.47	3.40	2.29	1.70	4.50	4.32	3.31	2.25	1.68
Horiz.	Down	90	10	6.09	5.35	2.79	1.43	0.94	10.07	8.19	3.41	1.57	1.00
		50	30	6.27	5.63	3.18	1.70	1.14	9.60	8.17	3.86	1.88	1.22
		50	10	6.61	5.90	3.27	1.73	1.15	11.15	9.27	4.09	1.93	1.24
		0	20	7.03	6.43	3.91	2.19	1.49	10.90	9.52	4.87	2.47	1.62
		0	10	7.31	6.66	4.00	2.22	1.51	11.97	10.32	5.08	2.52	1.64
		−50	20	7.73	7.20	4.77	2.85	1.99	11.64	10.49	6.02	3.25	2.18
		−50	10	8.09	7.52	4.91	2.89	2.01	12.98	11.56	6.36	3.34	2.22

[a]See Chapter 22, section Factors Affecting Heat Transfer across Air Spaces. Thermal resistance values were determined from the relation, $R = 1/C$, where $C = h_c + \varepsilon_{eff} h_r$. h_c is the conduction-convection coefficient, $\varepsilon_{eff} h_r$ is the radiation coefficient = $0.0068\varepsilon_{eff}[(t_m + 460)/100]^3$, and t_m is the mean temperature of the air space. Values for h_c were determined from data developed by Robinson et al. (1954). Equations (5) through (7) in Yarbrough (1983) show the data in this table in analytic form. For extrapolation from this table to air spaces less than 0.5 in. (as in insulating window glass), assume $h_c = 0.159(1 + 0.0016 t_m)/l$ where l is the air space thickness in inches, and h_c is heat transfer through the air space only.

[b]Values are based on data presented by Robinson et al. (1954). (Also see Chapter 3, Tables 3 and 4, and Chapter 36). Values apply for ideal conditions, i.e., air spaces of uniform thickness bounded by plane, smooth, parallel surfaces with no air leakage to or from the space. When accurate values are required, use overall U-factors deter-

mined through calibrated hot box (ASTM C 976) or guarded hot box (ASTM C 236) testing. Thermal resistance values for multiple air spaces must be based on careful estimates of mean temperature differences for each air space.

[c]A single resistance value cannot account for multiple air spaces; each air space requires a separate resistance calculation that applies only for the established boundary conditions. Resistances of horizontal spaces with heat flow downward are substantially independent of temperature difference.

[d]Interpolation is permissible for other values of mean temperature, temperature difference, and effective emittance ε_{eff}. Interpolation and moderate extrapolation for air spaces greater than 3.5 in. are also permissible.

[e]Effective emittance ε_{eff} of the air space is given by $1/\varepsilon_{eff} = 1/\varepsilon_1 + 1/\varepsilon_2 - 1$, where ε_1 and ε_2 are the emittances of the surfaces of the air space (see Table 2).

Table 4   Typical Thermal Properties of Common Building and Insulating Materials—Design Values[a] (Continued)

Description	Density, lb/ft³	Conductivity[b] (k), Btu·in / h·ft²·°F	Conductance (C), Btu / h·ft²·°F	Resistance[c] (R) Per Inch Thickness (1/k), °F·ft²·h / Btu·in	Resistance[c] (R) For Thickness Listed (1/C), °F·ft²·h / Btu	Specific Heat, Btu / lb·°F
Expanded polystyrene, extruded (smooth skin surface) (HCFC-142b exp.)[h]	1.8-3.5	0.20	—	5.00	—	0.29
Expanded polystyrene, molded beads	1.0	0.26	—	3.85	—	—
	1.25	0.25	—	4.00	—	—
	1.5	0.24	—	4.17	—	—
	1.75	0.24	—	4.17	—	—
	2.0	0.23	—	4.35	—	—
Cellular polyurethane/polyisocyanurate[i,l] (CFC-11 exp.) (unfaced)	1.5	0.16-0.18	—	6.25-5.56	—	0.38
Cellular polyisocyanurate[i] (CFC-11 exp.) (gas-permeable facers)	1.5-2.5	0.16-0.18	—	6.25-5.56	—	0.22
Cellular polyisocyanurate[j] (CFC-11 exp.) (gas-impermeable facers)	2.0	0.14	—	7.04	—	0.22
Cellular phenolic (closed cell) (CFC-11, CFC-113 exp.)[k]	3.0	0.12	—	8.20	—	—
Cellular phenolic (open cell)	1.8-2.2	0.23	—	4.40	—	—
Mineral fiber with resin binder	15.0	0.29	—	3.45	—	0.17
Mineral fiberboard, wet felted						
Core or roof insulation	16-17	0.34	—	2.94	—	—
Acoustical tile	18.0	0.35	—	2.86	—	0.19
Acoustical tile	21.0	0.37	—	2.70	—	—
Mineral fiberboard, wet molded						
Acoustical tile[l]	23.0	0.42	—	2.38	—	0.14
Wood or cane fiberboard						
Acoustical tile[l] ......0.5 in.	—	—	0.80	—	1.25	0.31
Acoustical tile[l] ......0.75 in.	—	—	0.53	—	1.89	—
Interior finish (plank, tile)	15.0	0.35	—	2.86	—	0.32
Cement fiber slabs (shredded wood with Portland cement binder)	25-27.0	0.50-0.53	—	2.0-1.89	—	—
Cement fiber slabs (shredded wood with magnesia oxysulfide binder)	22.0	0.57	—	1.75	—	0.31
Loose Fill						
Cellulosic insulation (milled paper or wood pulp)	2.3-3.2	0.27-0.32	—	3.70-3.13	—	0.33
Perlite, expanded	2.0-4.1	0.27-0.31	—	3.7-3.3	—	0.26
	4.1-7.4	0.31-0.36	—	3.3-2.8	—	—
	7.4-11.0	0.36-0.42	—	2.8-2.4	—	—
Mineral fiber (rock, slag, or glass)[g]						
approx. 3.75-5 in.	0.6-2.0	—	—	—	11.0	0.17
approx. 6.5-8.75 in.	0.6-2.0	—	—	—	19.0	—
approx. 7.5-10 in.	0.6-2.0	—	—	—	22.0	—
approx. 10.25-13.75 in.	0.6-2.0	—	—	—	30.0	—
Mineral fiber (rock, slag, or glass)[g]						
approx. 3.5 in. (closed sidewall application)	2.0-3.5	—	—	—	12.0-14.0	—
Vermiculite, exfoliated	7.0-8.2	0.47	—	2.13	—	0.32
	4.0-6.0	0.44	—	2.27	—	—
Spray Applied						
Polyurethane foam	1.5-2.5	0.16-0.18	—	6.25-5.56	—	—
Ureaformaldehyde foam	0.7-1.6	0.22-0.28	—	4.55-3.57	—	—
Cellulosic fiber	3.5-6.0	0.29-0.34	—	3.45-2.94	—	—
Glass fiber	3.5-4.5	0.26-0.27	—	3.85-3.70	—	—
Reflective Insulation						
Reflective material (ε < 0.5) in center of 3/4 in. cavity forms two 3/8 in. vertical air spaces[m]	—	—	0.31	—	3.2	—

METALS
(See Chapter 36, Table 3)

ROOFING

Asbestos-cement shingles	120	—	4.76	—	0.21	0.24
Asphalt roll roofing	70	—	6.50	—	0.15	0.36
Asphalt shingles	70	—	2.27	—	0.44	0.30
Built-up roofing ......0.375 in.	70	—	3.00	—	0.33	0.35
Slate ......0.5 in.	—	—	20.00	—	0.05	0.30
Wood shingles, plain and plastic film faced	—	—	1.06	—	0.94	0.31

PLASTERING MATERIALS

Cement plaster, sand aggregate	116	5.0	—	0.20	—	0.20
Sand aggregate ......0.375 in.	—	—	13.3	—	0.08	0.20
Sand aggregate ......0.75 in.	—	—	6.66	—	0.15	0.20

Table 4 Typical Thermal Properties of Common Building and Insulating Materials—Design Values[a] (Continued)

Description	Density, lb/ft^3	Conductivity[b] (k), Btu·in / h·ft^2·°F	Conductance (C), Btu / h·ft^2·°F	Resistance[c] (R) Per Inch Thickness (1/k), °F·ft^2·h / Btu·in	Resistance[c] (R) For Thickness Listed (1/C), °F·ft^2·h / Btu	Specific Heat, Btu / lb·°F
Gypsum plaster:						
Lightweight aggregate ....0.5 in.	45	—	3.12	—	0.32	—
Lightweight aggregate ....0.625 in.	45	—	2.67	—	0.39	—
Lightweight aggregate on metal lath ....0.75 in.	—	—	2.13	—	0.47	—
Perlite aggregate	45	1.5	—	0.67	—	0.32
Sand aggregate	105	5.6	—	0.18	—	0.20
Sand aggregate ....0.5 in.	105	—	11.10	—	0.09	—
Sand aggregate ....0.625 in.	105	—	9.10	—	0.11	—
Sand aggregate on metal lath ....0.75 in.	—	—	7.70	—	0.13	—
Vermiculite aggregate	45	1.7	—	0.59	—	—

MASONRY MATERIALS

Masonry Units

Description	Density, lb/ft^3	Conductivity[b] (k)	Conductance (C)	Resistance Per Inch (1/k)	Resistance For Thickness (1/C)	Specific Heat
Brick, fired clay	150	8.4-10.2	—	0.12-0.10	—	—
	140	7.4-9.0	—	0.14-0.11	—	—
	130	6.4-7.8	—	0.16-0.12	—	—
	120	5.6-6.8	—	0.18-0.15	—	0.19
	110	4.9-5.9	—	0.20-0.17	—	—
	100	4.2-5.1	—	0.24-0.20	—	—
	90	3.6-4.3	—	0.28-0.24	—	—
	80	3.0-3.7	—	0.33-0.27	—	—
	70	2.5-3.1	—	0.40-0.33	—	—
Clay tile, hollow						
1 cell deep ....3 in.	—	—	1.25	—	0.80	0.21
1 cell deep ....4 in.	—	—	0.90	—	1.11	—
2 cells deep...6 in.	—	—	0.66	—	1.52	—
2 cells deep...8 in.	—	—	0.54	—	1.85	—
2 cells deep...10 in.	—	—	0.45	—	2.22	—
3 cells deep...12 in.	—	—	0.40	—	2.50	—
Concrete blocks[n, o]						
Limestone aggregate						
8 in., 36 lb, 138 lb/ft^3 concrete, 2 cores	—	—	—	—	—	—
Same with perlite filled cores	—	—	0.48	—	2.1	—
12 in., 55 lb, 138 lb/ft^3 concrete, 2 cores	—	—	—	—	—	—
Same with perlite filled cores	—	—	0.27	—	3.7	—
Normal weight aggregate (sand and gravel)						
8 in., 33-36 lb, 126-136 lb/ft^3 concrete, 2 or 3 cores	—	—	0.90-1.03	—	1.11-0.97	0.22
Same with perlite filled cores	—	—	0.50	—	2.0	—
Same with vermiculite filled cores	—	—	0.52-0.73	—	1.92-1.37	—
12 in., 50 lb, 125 lb/ft^3 concrete, 2 cores	—	—	0.81	—	1.23	0.22
Medium weight aggregate (combinations of normal weight and lightweight aggregate)						
8 in., 26-29 lb, 97-112 lb/ft^3 concrete, 2 or 3 cores..	—	—	0.58-0.78	—	1.71-1.28	—
Same with perlite filled cores	—	—	0.27-0.44	—	3.7-2.3	—
Same with vermiculite filled cores	—	—	0.30	—	3.3	—
Same with molded EPS (beads) filled cores.........	—	—	0.32	—	3.2	—
Same with molded EPS inserts in cores...............	—	—	0.37	—	2.7	—
Lightweight aggregate (expanded shale, clay, slate or slag, pumice)						
6 in., 16-17 lb 85-87 lb/ft^3 concrete, 2 or 3 cores	—	—	0.52-0.61	—	1.93-1.65	—
Same with perlite filled cores	—	—	0.24	—	4.2	—
Same with vermiculite filled cores	—	—	0.33	—	3.0	—
8 in., 19-22 lb, 72-86 lb/ft^3 concrete	—	—	0.32-0.54	—	3.2-1.90	0.21
Same with perlite filled cores	—	—	0.15-0.23	—	6.8-4.4	—
Same with vermiculite filled cores	—	—	0.19-0.26	—	5.3-3.9	—
Same with molded EPS (beads) filled cores.........	—	—	0.21	—	4.8	—
Same with UF foam filled cores	—	—	0.22	—	4.5	—
Same with molded EPS inserts in cores...............	—	—	0.29	—	3.5	—
12 in., 32-36 lb, 80-90 lb/ft^3 concrete, 2 or 3 cores...	—	—	0.38-0.44	—	2.6-2.3	—
Same with perlite filled cores	—	—	0.11-0.16	—	9.2-6.3	—
Same with vermiculite filled cores	—	—	0.17	—	5.8	—
Stone, lime, or sand...	180	72	—	0.01	—	—
Quartzitic and sandstone	160	43	—	0.02	—	—
	140	24	—	0.04	—	—
	120	13	—	0.08	—	0.19
Calcitic, dolomitic, limestone, marble, and granite	180	30	—	0.03	—	—
	160	22	—	0.05	—	—
	140	16	—	0.06	—	—
	120	11	—	0.09	—	0.19
	100	8	—	0.13	—	—

Table 4   Typical Thermal Properties of Common Building and Insulating Materials—Design Values[a] (Continued)

Description	Density, lb/ft³	Conductivity[b] (k), Btu·in h·ft²·°F	Conductance (C), Btu h·ft²·°F	Resistance[c] (R) Per Inch Thickness (1/k), °F·ft²·h Btu·in	Resistance[c] (R) For Thickness Listed (1/C), °F·ft²·h Btu	Specific Heat, Btu lb·°F
Gypsum partition tile						
3 by 12 by 30 in., solid	—	—	0.79	—	1.26	0.19
3 by 12 by 30 in., 4 cells	—	—	0.74	—	1.35	—
4 by 12 by 30 in., 3 cells	—	—	0.60	—	1.67	—
Concretes[i]						
Sand and gravel or stone aggregate concretes (concretes	150	10.0-20.0	—	0.10-0.05	—	—
with more than 50% quartz or quartzite sand have	140	9.0-18.0	—	0.11-0.06	—	0.19-0.24
conductivities in the higher end of the range)	130	7.0-13.0	—	0.14-0.08	—	—
Limestone concretes	140	11.1	—	0.09	—	—
	120	7.9	—	0.13	—	—
	100	5.5	—	0.18	—	—
Gypsum-fiber concrete (87.5% gypsum, 12.5% wood chips)	51	1.66	—	0.60	—	0.21
Cement/lime, mortar, and stucco	120	9.7	—	0.10	—	—
	100	6.7	—	0.15	—	—
	80	4.5	—	0.22	—	—
Lightweight aggregate concretes						
Expanded shale, clay, or slate; expanded slags;	120	6.4-9.1	—	0.16-0.11	—	—
cinders; pumice (with density up to 100 lb/ft³); and	100	4.7-6.2	—	0.21-0.16	—	0.20
scoria (sanded concretes have conductivities in the	80	3.3-4.1	—	0.30-0.24	—	0.20
higher end of the range)	60	2.1-2.5	—	0.48-0.40	—	—
	40	1.3	—	0.78	—	—
Perlite, vermiculite, and polystyrene beads	50	1.8-1.9	—	0.55-0.53	—	—
	40	1.4-1.5	—	0.71-0.67	—	0.15-0.23
	30	1.1	—	0.91	—	—
	20	0.8	—	1.25	—	—
Foam concretes	120	5.4	—	0.19	—	—
	100	4.1	—	0.24	—	—
	80	3.0	—	0.33	—	—
	70	2.5	—	0.40	—	—
Foam concretes and cellular concretes	60	2.1	—	0.48	—	—
	40	1.4	—	0.71	—	—
	20	0.8	—	1.25	—	—
SIDING MATERIALS (on flat surface)						
Shingles						
Asbestos-cement	120	—	4.75	—	0.21	—
Wood, 16 in., 7.5 exposure	—	—	1.15	—	0.87	0.31
Wood, double, 16-in., 12-in. exposure	—	—	0.84	—	1.19	0.28
Wood, plus ins. backer board, 0.312 in.	—	—	0.71	—	1.40	0.31
Siding						
Asbestos-cement, 0.25 in., lapped	—	—	4.76	—	0.21	0.24
Asphalt roll siding	—	—	6.50	—	0.15	0.35
Asphalt insulating siding (0.5 in. bed.)	—	—	0.69	—	1.46	0.35
Hardboard siding, 0.4375 in.	—	—	1.49	—	0.67	0.28
Wood, drop, 1 by 8 in.	—	—	1.27	—	0.79	0.28
Wood, bevel, 0.5 by 8 in., lapped	—	—	1.23	—	0.81	0.28
Wood, bevel, 0.75 by 10 in., lapped	—	—	0.95	—	1.05	0.28
Wood, plywood, 0.375 in., lapped	—	—	1.69	—	0.59	0.29
Aluminum, steel, or vinyl[p, q], over sheathing						
Hollow-backed	—	—	1.64	—	0.61	0.29[q]
Insulating-board backed nominal 0.375 in.	—	—	0.55	—	1.82	0.32
Insulating-board backed nominal 0.375 in., foil backed	—	—	0.34	—	2.96	—
Architectural (soda-lime float) glass	158	6.9	—	—	—	0.21
WOODS (12% moisture content)[e,f]						
Hardwoods						0.39[s]
Oak	41.2-46.8	1.12-1.25	—	0.89-0.80	—	
Birch	42.6-45.4	1.16-1.22	—	0.87-0.82	—	
Maple	39.8-44.0	1.09-1.19	—	0.92-0.84	—	
Ash	38.4-41.9	1.06-1.14	—	0.94-0.88	—	
Softwoods						0.39[s]
Southern Pine	35.6-41.2	1.00-1.12	—	1.00-0.89	—	
Douglas Fir-Larch	33.5-36.3	0.95-1.01	—	1.06-0.99	—	
Southern Cypress	31.4-32.1	0.90-0.92	—	1.11-1.09	—	
Hem-Fir, Spruce-Pine-Fir	24.5-31.4	0.74-0.90	—	1.35-1.11	—	
West Coast Woods, Cedars	21.7-31.4	0.68-0.90	—	1.48-1.11	—	
California Redwood	24.5-28.0	0.74-0.82	—	1.35-1.22	—	

INDEX

Tables, Maps, and Forms